T0030774

Men-at-Arms • 545

Medieval Indian Armies (1)

Hindu, Buddhist and Jain

David Nicolle • Illustrated by Graham Turner

Series editors Martin Windrow & Nick Reynolds

OSPREY PUBLISHING
Bloomsbury Publishing Plc
Kemp House, Chawley Park, Cumnor Hill, Oxford OX2 9PH, UK
29 Earlsfort Terrace, Dublin 2, Ireland
1385 Broadway, 5th Floor, New York, NY 10018, USA
E-mail: info@ospreypublishing.com
www.ospreypublishing.com

OSPREY is a trademark of Osprey Publishing Ltd

First published in Great Britain in 2022

© Osprey Publishing Ltd, 2022

All rights reserved. No part of this publication may be reproduced or transmitted in any form or by any means, electronic or mechanical, including photocopying, recording, or any information storage or retrieval system, without prior permission in writing from the publishers.

A catalogue record for this book is available from the British Library.

ISBN: PB 9781472843449; eBook 9781472843463;
ePDF 9781472843456; XML 9781472843470

22 23 24 25 26   10 9 8 7 6 5 4 3 2 1

Index by Rob Munro
Typeset by PDQ Digital Media Solutions, Bungay, UK
Printed and bound in India by Replika Press Private Ltd.

Osprey Publishing supports the Woodland Trust, the UK's leading woodland conservation charity.

To find out more about our authors and books visit www.ospreypublishing.com. Here you will find extracts, author interviews, details of forthcoming events and the option to sign up for our newsletter.

Dedication

For Lisa Priya and Charlotte Isla, 'casting a golden glow over the declining years'.

Author's note

India is often described as a subcontinent because of its size and variety of climates and seasons, but where Indian history is concerned there is also the question of how far Indian civilization spread and what therefore counted as 'India'. For the purposes of this book 'medieval India' will cover India, Pakistan, Bangladesh, Nepal and parts of Afghanistan, but will exclude Sri Lanka, Burma, the East Indies and Indo-China.

Editor's note

Unless otherwise credited, all illustrations are from the author's collection.

Artist's note

Readers may care to note that the original paintings from which the colour plates in this book were prepared are available for private sale. All reproduction copyright whatsoever is retained by the publishers. All enquiries should be addressed to:

graham@studio88.co.uk

The publishers regret that they can enter into no correspondence upon this matter.

Title-page illustration: Carving of confronted cavalrymen, one riding an armoured horse, on the exterior of the Chennakesava Temple, built in 1268 at Somanathapura, Karnataka.

Back-cover drawing: Hero stone of the Mukkanna Udaiyar period, Vijayanagar 15th to 17th centuries, from Anandur, Dharapuri.

MEDIEVAL INDIAN ARMIES (1)

HINDU, BUDDHIST AND JAIN

INTRODUCTION

While some medieval Chinese scholars referred to 'five Indias' even within the Indian subcontinent, some studies of medieval Indian costume have overstated the similarity between the north and south, focusing on a common culture which tended towards uniformity and too often overlooking the climatic differences which made for variety.

Other difficulties arise from the fact that some on the nationalist wing of Indian scholarship still regard the medieval period as one of Hindu failure in the face of Islamic aggression. In fact there was no lack of courage or commitment on the part of Hindu, Buddhist and Jain rulers and peoples. Nevertheless, some attribute Muslim military success to political failures by non-Islamic rulers, ignoring comparable fragmentation on the Muslim side, and to a straightforward inferiority in military structures, armaments, organization and tactics. One scholar even summarized these centuries by suggesting that the fall of Hindu society was the outcome of cultural and political suicide rather than murder (Prakash 1962: 115–17).

Then there is the question of the Indian caste system, which was fundamental to traditional Hindu religious beliefs and social structures. It has also been widely blamed for medieval Hindu political and military failures when compared to the theoretical egalitarianism of Islamic civilization. What is clear is that, unlike most previous invaders, the Muslims did not integrate into Hindu civilization, but remained separate and distinct while striving for political and cultural domination.

After the Europeans arrived, most notably the British, their racist and imperialist beliefs led them to divide the pre-European states between supposedly aggressive, intolerant, masculine and 'active' Muslims, and tolerant, civilized, meek and 'passive' Hindus. More recently, some historians have tended to overlook the warlike elements in traditional Indian culture, rooted in Hindu religious epics. Particularly insidious has been a focus on the so-called ethnicity of various Indian peoples; a primary distinction being drawn between earlier Dravidian peoples, now mostly living in southern India but including residual populations further north, and the supposedly Indo-Aryan peoples of northern India, descended from Eurasian steppe invaders.

Hero stones can be found outside some Indian villages where they are still venerated by having wildflowers pushed into their carvings, this example being at the southern edge of Muthagadahalli, east of Nagalapura in Karnataka.

CHRONOLOGY

*c.*300–888	Pallava state in southern and south-eastern India.
*c.*320–550	Gupta Empire in northern India.
*c.*454	First Huna (Hephthalite or Sweta Huna) invasion of northern India.
*c.*495	Second Huna (Alchon Huns) invasion of north-western India.
*c.*500–*c.*1000	Pandya state in eastern coastal Deccan.
*c.*540	Collapse of the Gupta Empire.
543–757	First Chalukya dynasty (Chalukyas of Vatapi) in central and western Deccan.
622	*Hijra* (emigration) of Prophet Muhammad from Mecca to Madina (start of Islamic 'Hijri' era).
624–1189	Eastern Chalukya dynasty (Chalukyas of Vengi) on eastern coast of India and eastern Deccan.
625–855	Karkota state in Kashmir.
665–870	Turk Shahi state in eastern Afghanistan and northern Pakistan.
712	Muslim Arab conquest of Sindh.
753–982	Rashtrakuta state in Deccan and beyond.
*c.*750–*c.*1100	Gurjara-Pratihara state in Bengal and central northern India.
*c.*760–1142	Pala Empire in Bengal and Bihar.
*c.*800–*c.*1200	Minor dynasties in fragmented northern Deccan and central northern India.
842	Break-up of Tibetan Empire.
850–1026	Hindu-Shahi state in eastern Afghanistan and western Punjab.
*c.*850–1279	Cola state in southern India.
854–1011	Habbari Arab Amirate in Sindh.
*c.*940–1244	Chaulukya state in Rajasthan and Gujarat.
973–1189	Western Chaulukya Empire in west and central Deccan.
977–1186	Ghaznavid Empire in Afghanistan, eastern Iran, Islamic Central Asia and north-western India.

1001–1027	Ghaznavid raids and conquests in north-western India (Pakistan).
1026–1356	Soomra (Shi'a Muslim) state in Sindh.
1070–1230	Sena Empire in northern and north-eastern India.
1089–1197	Gahadavala state in central northern India.
*c.*1100–1343	Hoysala state (Empire from 1187) in southern Deccan.
*c.*1190–1294	Yadava Devagiri state in northern Deccan.
1191	First Battle of Tarain; Chahamana King Prithiviraj Chauhan and his allies defeat Muslim Ghurid ruler Mu'izz al-Din.
1192	Second Battle of Tarain; Ghurid ruler Mu'izz al-Din defeats Chahamanas and their allies.
1192–93	Conquest of Delhi by Ghurid general, Qutb al-Din Aybak.
1200	Conquest of Bihar and Bengal by Sultan Ikhtiyar al-Din Bakhtiyar Khalji.
1216–1327	Later Pandya state in southern India.
1221	Chingiz Khan forces the last Khwarazmian Shah, Jalal al-Din Mangburni, to retreat into north-western India.
1231	Death of Khwarazmian Shah Jalal al-Din in present-day Turkey.
1226	Establishment of the Delhi Sultanate – under five sequential dynasties: Mamluks, 1226–90; Khaljis, 1290–1320; Tughlaqs, 1320–1414; Sayyids, 1414–51; and Lodis, 1451–1526.
1310–11	Siege of Hoysala capital of Dwarasamudra (now Halebidu) by Delhi Sultanate general Malik Kafur.
1336–1524	Samma state (Muslim) in Sindh and neighbouring regions.
1336–1576	Sultanate of Bengal, at its greatest extent including Bangladesh, Bihar and parts of north-eastern India.

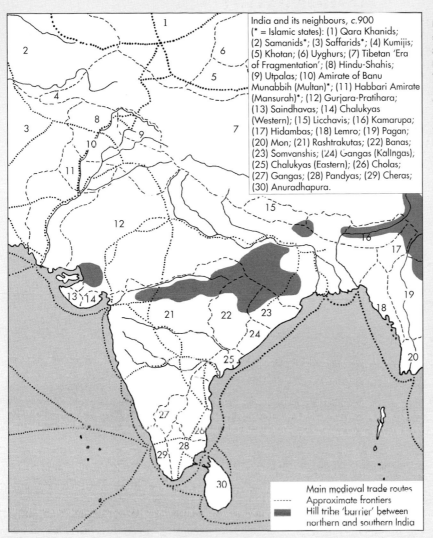

India and its neighbours, c.900
(* = Islamic states): (1) Qara Khanids;
(2) Samanids*; (3) Saffarids*; (4) Kumijis;
(5) Khotan; (6) Uyghurs; (7) Tibetan 'Era
of Fragmentation'; (8) Hindu-Shahis;
(9) Utpalas; (10) Amirate of Banu
Munabbih (Multan)*; (11) Habbari Amirate
(Mansurah)*; (12) Gurjara-Pratihara;
(13) Saindhavas; (14) Chalukyas
(Western); (15) Licchavis; (16) Kamarupa;
(17) Hidambas; (18) Lemro; (19) Pagan;
(20) Mon; (21) Rashtrakutas; (22) Banas;
(23) Somvanshis; (24) Gangas (Kalingas);
(25) Chalukyas (Eastern); (26) Cholas;
(27) Gangas; (28) Pandyas; (29) Cheras;
(30) Anuradhapura.

Main medieval trade routes
Approximate frontiers
Hill tribe 'barrier' between
northern and southern India

Much of India resembled a scattering of agricultural zones within valleys separated by jungles or mountains. There was great variety in Indian climates and seasons. The rains and heat of summer made campaigning virtually impossible from May to September; the best campaigning season was October and November when crops were ripe and green, making it possible for troops and their animals to live off the land. Other geographical factors included the relatively narrow strategic corridor between the Indus and Ganges plains, bounded by desert to the south and mountains to the north; other smaller strategic passes could decide the fate of even the best-prepared armies. Forests, rivers and marshes were similarly significant in several regions, while hill tribes whose territory extended from Kutch and Rajasthan to Orissa remained an obstacle to invasion southwards from the Indus–Ganges plain to the Deccan.

1336–1646	Vijayanagara Empire in southern Deccan and southern India.
1346–1589	Sultanate of Kashmir in north-western India.
1347–1527	Bahmanid Sultanate in northern and western Deccan.
1353–54	First invasion of Bengal by Sultan Firuz Shah Tughluq of Delhi.
1359	Second invasion of Bengal by Sultan Firuz Shah Tughluq of Delhi.
1382–1601	Faruqi Sultanate in west-central India.
1391–1583	Sultanate of Gujarat in western India.
1394–1479	Sultanate of Jaunpur in north-central India.
1398	Timur-i Lenk (Tamerlane) invades Sultanate of Delhi; seizes, sacks and temporarily occupies Delhi.
1401–1531	Sultanate of Malwa in west-central India.
1526	Zahir al-Din Muhammad Babur defeats the last Lodi Sultan of Delhi at the battle of Panipat and establishes the Mughul Empire in India.

POLITICAL SYSTEMS AND FRAGMENTATION

Indian *varna* or castes formed a class system based upon the supposed ethnicity of a family, as was the case in many civilizations, but in Hindu India this was justified by religion. *Brahmins* formed the highest and primarily priestly caste while the role of the *kshatriya* caste was government and warfare. By medieval times the *kshatriya* were effectively equal or even superior to the *brahmins* in terms of power while retaining some ancient privileges including 'marriage by capture' or permitting women to choose their husbands freely. Third in rank was the *vaisha* merchant caste. The lowest of the four main *varna* were the *shudra*, while below them were those who fell outside the caste system. It has been suggested that India's caste system reached a peak of rigidity by the late 12th century, with rulers regarding it as their duty to punish 'sinful' meddling with the existing structure. On the other hand, *brahmins* could be warriors or even bandits and many *kshatriya* also participated in trade. Then there were cases where entire castes could rise in status, such as the *Jats* who, widely regarded as *vaisha* or even *shudra*, could proclaim themselves as *kshatriya*.

In many respects clothing, hairstyles and the carrying of weapons proclaimed caste – long hair theoretically being the mark of *brahmins*, *kshatriya* and the wealthiest *vaisha*. For example, an extremely detailed description of a wealthy Kashmiri in the late 8th or early 9th century stated that his hair was five *angulis* (1 *anguli* = three finger widths) long and was tied in a thick topknot called a *chudah*; the man also wore a sharp-edged ivory comb in his hair (Chandra 1960: 3).

In practice, military recruitment was drawn from a far broader pool of manpower, though the *kshatriya* remained a military and commanding elite. Virtually all castes and ethnicities would eventually be involved, along with Muslims and foreigners. The central Hindu belief in almost endless reincarnation answered the problems this raised by suggesting such recruits had been *kshatriya* in a former life, had then fallen from grace but could be received back into the 'Aryan fold' by making penitentiary sacrifices. In fact, many Rajput families who fought against Muslim domination after the medieval period were probably descended from such outsiders or foreigners.

Within the traditional system, a ruler's coronation oath was made to a god or gods, not to the people, and they were in no sense constitutional monarchs. On the other hand, the idea that Hindu rulers in southern India were sacred 'god-kings' is misleading, for rulers remained indebted to the gods for their status and 'within the realm of men'. The *brahmin* caste continued in its priestly role while the king, as a *kshatriya*, remained the gift-giving hero-warrior, more or less following traditional advice that half of his tax income should be spent on military matters.

According to ancient Indian theories of government, a ruler's senior ministers – his *ratnins* or 'jewels' – included the *senani* or commander-in-chief and the *suta*, who seems originally to have been commander of the chariot corps. Other officials ranged from the *gramani*, who may originally have been prominent village headmen selected as a council of ministers, to the *bhagadhuk*, a tax collector or finance minister, and the

The heritage of armour in India. (A) Ivory carving of a warrior excavated in Patna, possibly Mauryan, 3rd–2nd centuries BC or later; now held at the Patna State Museum of Bihar, inv. no. 991.1936. (B) Carving known as *Catubhuji Bhagavan*, traditionally identified as four-armed Vishnu, though it might actually represent an attendant of that god; found at Malhar in Madhya Pradesh, perhaps 1st century BC; now held at the Government Museum, Mathura, no. 15.956. (C) *The Army of Mara*, Gandharan carving from an unknown location, 3rd or 4th century; Central Museum, Lahore, inv. nr. G-78 (old 538).

samgrahita, or treasurer. During the medieval period a council of state remained central to Hindu government, but varied in size and structure between kingdoms. In most cases the senior minister was the *pradhana*, seconded by a war minister whose title varied but who was expected to be expert in the theory and practice of war and administration. He ensured that fortresses were garrisoned and the army was equipped and trained. As active soldiers, most were *kshatriya*, but could be *brahmins*.

Several dynasties attempted to dominate and unify the country as part of a generally accepted policy of military competition between rulers. Following the decline of the Gupta Empire in the late 5th and early 6th centuries, however, India remained fragmented while pressure from powerful neighbours, almost invariably from the north-west, remained the norm. Nevertheless, the degree of Sassanian Persian control over much of Afghanistan and Pakistan between the 3rd and 6th centuries remains a matter of debate, though Sassanian cultural and military influence is clear both here and deeper into India.

Equally important were the Huna invasions of the late 5th and early 6th centuries, which tore parts of north-western Pakistan away from the mainstream of Indian civilization for centuries. Nor were Sassanian Persians, Hunas and other Central Asian peoples alone in threatening India. In the mid-7th century Tibetans, in alliance with T'ang China and Nepal, invaded and temporarily held several areas. Then came the Muslim Arabs in the later 7th century, followed by notably more successful Turkish-Muslim invaders from the 11th century onwards.

Events on the frontiers had an impact upon regions deeper within India and it has been argued that towns across the Ganges plain went into decline during the early-medieval period, only reviving under Muslim control from the 11th century onwards. Meanwhile a number of extensive, powerful and sometimes astonishingly wealthy states emerged in various parts of India, ranging from the Palas and Pratiharas in the north to the Rashtrakutas and Western Chalukyas within peninsular India.

Rivalry between such dynasties could be ferocious and did not disappear in the face of Islamic invasion, some Hindu princes allying themselves with Muslim sultans against local rivals during the 12th century. This was followed by a period of even greater upheaval in northern and central India during the 14th, 15th and 16th centuries, causing large numbers of Hindu warriors, artisan and peasant communities to move around the country in search of new employment or new land. Paradoxically, this led to the settlement of territories between the old core areas of Hindu civilization and the emergence of new political centres around newly fortified towns. Dominant Muslim dynasties were not alone in benefiting from such changes; the Vijayanagara kings of the deep south rising as a new and successful bastion of Hindu resistance from the later medieval period onwards (1336–1646).

Another interesting aspect of medieval Hindu civilization was its acceptance of the inevitability of conflict, from the state to the local level. This can be seen in the *smritis*, or secondary Hindu religious texts, which provided a basis for life and government. Several such *smritis* declared that a strong king was permitted to declare war upon a weaker neighbour for even a minor reason, though the resulting conflict had to be carried out according to accepted rules. As a counter-balance, weaker rulers were urged to seek security through reliable alliances.

(D) *Dvarapala* (door guardian), left of the entrance to a Buddhist cave temple at the Pitalkhora Caves, Maharashtra, and now destroyed. (E) *Dvarapala*, right of the entrance of the same temple. (F) *The Army of Mara*, Gandharan-Kushan from an unknown location, late 2nd or early 3rd century; now held at the Freer Gallery of Art, Washington, DC, inv. 49.9.

Decorative tile from a Buddhist *stupa* (sepulchral monument) at Harwan in Indian-administered Kashmir, 4th–5th centuries. It is now held at the Musée Guimet, Paris, France.

The rules of statecraft not only permitted attack at any time and under all circumstances, but allowed that enemy lands could be devastated, trees cut down, crops and stores burned and inhabitants taken into captivity. When added to the *kshatriya* caste's abhorrence of dying in bed rather than on the battlefield, the result was chronic warfare. Successful conquerors were nevertheless urged to be satisfied with payment of tribute and formal submission rather than annexing too much of their enemy's lands or – worse still – disrupting its administration. In fact, the 7th-century Chinese traveller Xuanzang (Hiuen-Tsang) noted that Indian warfare, though frequent, did little harm to the country. The treasure, armaments and provisions of a defeated king became the winner's property, however, with little reference to a sharing of booty among the troops, as was characteristic of traditional Islamic rules of war.

There were also rules about the treatment of the enemy. A foe who laid down his weapons, threw himself upon the mercy of the conqueror or was wounded should not be killed. The same applied to those fleeing a battlefield, while injured prisoners were to be treated by the victorious army's doctors but, while such advice had supposedly been followed in ancient times, it may have been less characteristic of the medieval period.

The ancient Indian philosopher Chanakya (Kautilya) advised in his *Arthashastra* political treatise that, while a powerful ruler should follow the *dharmayudha* chivalrous code, a weaker ruler could use all means fair or foul if he was subject to aggression. The *Arthashastra* probably reached its final form in the 3rd century and thereafter continued to have a profound influence, so it is not surprising that many medieval southern

Indian rulers violated the accepted rules of war when hard-pressed. Even so, the fact that Hindu, Jain or Buddhist states shared many basic religious values meant that their rivalries were primarily political – if violent. It was only with the coming of Islam that deeper religious differences added intensity to conflicts between non-Muslim and Muslim rulers.

At the other end of the scale of conflict, cattle raiding was deeply rooted in Hindu Vedic tradition and continued to be a major problem across India. Indeed, quarrels between villages usually took the form of stealing cows, though this may often have been the result rather the cause of such disputes. Cattle rustling was even seen as a proper method of declaring war or initiating a conflict between rulers.

CULTURAL DIVERSITY AND UNITY

Cultural complexity within India was not solely a result of the Muslim conquests, however. Buddhism and Buddhist states were already in decline, accompanied by a Hindu revival, along with the emergence of Jain-ruled states and the arrival of a Parsee (Zoroastrian) community. The fluctuating fortunes of pre-colonial Christian and Jewish minorities were another feature of the medieval period, along with the continued presence of animist or only superficially Hindu tribal peoples in the forests and hills.

Meanwhile, Hinduism and Buddhism flourished beyond the north-western frontiers of India for a long time, though eventually superseded by massive conversion to Islam. In fact, Indian culture and influence had spread deep into Central Asian regions, which would become almost

ABOVE LEFT
Dating from the 2nd–3rd centuries, this stone architectural decoration in the form of an elephant and warrior was taken from an abandoned Buddhist monastery at Tapa-i Kafariha in Afghanistan. It is now held at the Musee Guimet, Paris, France.

ABOVE RIGHT
Bronze statuette of a cavalryman, Alxon-Hunnic, late 5th century, from northern Afghanistan or Tajikistan. U. Jäger photograph. (Courtesy of the Pritzker Family)

These four armoured men in early Indian terracotta statuettes are sometimes identified as 'foreign warriors' because they are wearing armour. At the top, Kushan, 1st–4th centuries, now in the Baroda Museum and Picture Gallery, Vadodara, India; second and third images, Kushan, 2nd–3rd centuries, now in the Indian Museum, Kolkata; at bottom, Gupta, 3rd-4th centuries.

entirely Islamic by the close of the medieval period. Buddhism would remain strong in western Turkestan until the 9th century, retaining strong links to northern India, especially Kashmir and those parts of northern Pakistan where Buddhism flourished even longer. Beyond the mountains lay the flourishing oasis of Khotan which had probably been colonized by both Indians and Chinese in the 3rd century BC. In fact, the Khotanese language, related to Sughdian, Persian and Sanskrit, used a variation of the Indian alphabet. South of the mountains in Pakistan's Tochi Valley, inscriptions using the Greek alphabet introduced by Alexander the Great in the 4th century BC, have been found to date from as late as the 8th century.

It is now clear that new Buddhist sites were being established in Afghanistan's Bamiyan Valley well into the 7th and 8th centuries at a time when Buddhism was once thought to have declined in this area. Instead, Buddhist and Hindu civilization seems to have strengthened and spread, achieving a final flowering during the first three centuries of the Islamic era – even after neighbouring regions fell to Arab–Islamic conquest.

How much influence these cultures had upon subsequent Islamic civilization, including military institutions, remains unclear. Meanwhile the presence of non-Muslims, including large numbers of Hindu soldiers and their families, within Islamic realms has long been recognized. What is perhaps more surprising was the presence of Muslim communities within regions yet to fall to Islamic conquest.

The province of Sindh in southern Pakistan is of particular interest in this context. Here the first official Muslim invading army under the military commander Muhammad Ibn Qasim found considerable support among the Buddhist-majority population against Raja Dahir, the province's ruler (r. 695–712), and even some support among the Hindu military elite. Further north, Kashmir would survive as a bastion of Buddhist and Hindu resistance to Islamic conquest even after the Hindu-Shahi dynasty were forced to abandon their territories in Afghanistan and north-western Pakistan. The neighbouring Himalayan territory of Ladakh was too remote to play a major role in these struggles, but its isolation also meant that 12th- and 13th-century wall-paintings survive in the Buddhist monastery at Alchi, illustrating costume, arms, armour, horse-harness and a host of other details.

Medieval India's contacts with the outside world were not solely in the hands of Indian or Muslim merchants, invaders and settlers. The role of long-established Jewish and Christian communities was important, with the medieval Jewish community in India maintaining close links with Iraq and Yemen, both of which had substantial Jewish minorities dating from long before the Islamic era. One 13th-century inscribed copper plate from the Kochi area of Kerala actually referred to a Jewish merchant named Issuppu Irappan (Joseph Rabban) in the context of a toll levied on trade in horses and perhaps elephants. Both the Nestorian and Syriac Christian communities in India had Middle Eastern roots as a result of trade links and missionary activity, recent archaeological research showing that an Arab Christian community located in what are now Kuwait, the Gulf coast of Saudi Arabia, Qatar, the United Arab Emirates and northern Oman flourished well into the Islamic period. They would have formed a vital element in the network of trade routes and ports linking India with the Middle East and Mediterranean world.

The cultural harmony of medieval India should not be overstated. For example, the Hindu King Harsha of Kashmir (r. 1089–1101), desperately short of cash to maintain his army, was accused of despoiling the temples and robbing their treasures – in other words, he taxed them more heavily than was thought right. For many centuries, competition between Hindus, Buddhists and Jains had only occasionally taken the form of open warfare, but the rise of 'warrior ascetics' led to religious clashes, for example between Jains and Hindus in 12th-century Karnataka. Interdenominational conflict would of course become worse following the rise of the Islamic Delhi Sultanate, with economic rivalry often given religious sanction.

Then there was the question of who was considered an insider and who an outsider within the Hindu ethical system. The basic Sanskrit term for an outsider, barbarian or foreigner was *mleccha*. Such people not only included foreign invaders but also many of India's indigenous tribal peoples. *Mlecchas* were not necessarily regarded as being inferior, but were perceived to be different and should therefore be kept apart from higher-caste Hindu society. Nevertheless, many *mlecchas*, incomers or indigenous, possessed useful skills and were therefore recruited into state service as soldiers and especially as spies because they were often able to cross frontiers without attracting too much attention.

The position of Arabs was further complicated by the fact that they came from the west, from the same direction as Alexander the Great. Though considered *mlecchas*, they were often called *yavanas* – a word earlier used to describe Alexander's Macedonians and Greeks. The Hindu concept of *mleccha* left open the possibility of assimilation into Indian society, especially if those concerned adopted Indian dress, language, manners and diet. Because they resisted doing so, however, and in fact strove to maintain themselves as a conquering elite, Muslims remained *mlecchas* for much longer than their predecessors. The egalitarian fundamentals of Islam also made it difficult for Muslims to conform to Hindu ideas of *varna* or caste and in fact the majority of Indian converts to Islam are believed to have come from the lowest castes.

Over millennia, the *brahmin* caste developed a philosophy of patient accommodation built upon a belief that invaders arrived and either left or were absorbed into *Aryavarta* (the abode of the Aryans). Here, it was believed, the divinely ordained system would endure until the end of the current cycle of time. This concept did not work with invading Muslim *mlecchas*, however, who steadfastly refused to be absorbed into the existing Hindu structure of society. Furthermore, India's new Muslim rulers were contemptuous of the Hindu world view. Meanwhile, evidence of increasing changing of castes, or what would now be called social mobility, was widely seen as evidence of the approaching Age of Kali when a breakdown of the divine order would precede doomsday and the destruction of the universe. Faced with such a prospect, much of the *brahmin* elite withdrew from worldly affairs into mystical contemplation.

The Indian historian Ashirbadi Lal Srivastava has argued that demoralization played a major role in Hindu political and military defeats during the medieval period. Such defeatism was strengthened by a profound belief in fate – that it was better to submit to a powerful opponent rather than cause anarchy. Religious texts were found to support such views, including a passage in the *Mahabharata* which stated

Carved architectural fragment from the Hindu temple at Bhumara in Madhya Pradesh, Gupta period, *c.*5th century. Now held at the Indian Museum, Kolkata, inv. NS4934-A25059.

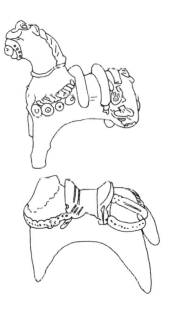

Terracotta horses. Above, toy horse with full harness and an early form of framed saddle, excavated at Khkari Baba Dherai, a largely Kushan site in the Peshawar Valley but perhaps as late as the 6th century. Below, toy horse with a later form of framed saddle having a flared cantle, found in the 8th–12th-centuries archaeological levels at Tulumba, in the Punjab.

Terracotta plaque or architectural decoration showing the God Rama, from the northern Indian state of Haryana, possibly from Nachar Khera, 5th century.

BELOW LEFT
Buddhist wall-paintings of cavalrymen aboard a stylized boat in cave 17 at Ajanta, Maharashtra state, India, late 5th century.

BELOW RIGHT
Foot soldiers with reverse-curved swords and large shields in front of a saddled horse depicted in cave 17 at Ajanta, Maharashtra state, India, late 5th century.

that the people should go forward to receive the invader with respect. Furthermore, this passage in the sacred text maintained that there was no greater evil than anarchy.

This left Hinduism's second caste, the *kshatriya*, to develop a philosophy of heroic resistance and an epic literature built upon the traditions of the warrior Rajputs. This bardic culture reached a pinnacle during the 11th and 12th centuries, with the writing of several remarkable *carita-kavyas* or 'accounts of heroes'. Renowned bards and minstrels are known to have moved around the country, singing songs of valour and resistance in which the relatively restrained language of earlier times was replaced by celebration of a fierce and arrogant warrior elite. One 12th-century example from the Malwa area proclaimed that when famed Chaulukya ruler Jayasimha Siddharaja became king (r. *c.*1092–*c.*1142), his bravery shone like a volcano emerging from beneath the sea, raising waves like those which will one day overwhelm the world (Yadava 2001: 68).

Hindu culture became almost militaristic during this period. Yet the contempt for death supposedly characteristic of the higher castes may have had negative military consequences. A belief that victory depended upon the favour of the gods was certainly not confined to Indian civilization, but Hinduism may have taken this further, regarding battle as a huge religious rite which required proper purification beforehand. Added to this was a more-than-usually profound belief in astrology, with the day and time of combat being selected by astrologers. Booty and glory were of course promised to the victor, along with a superior reincarnation for those who fell in battle increasingly seen as the best outcome for a member of the warrior elite.

Heroes slain in battle would be welcomed into heaven by the 14 families of *Apsaras*, female spirits of the clouds and waters. Capture, especially by Muslims, was a disaster and even if a man escaped to return to own people, he was supposedly never fully accepted back into his caste.

For medieval European visitors such as Marco Polo, who had virtually no understanding of the basics of Hindu belief, the contempt for death shown by southern Indian warriors contrasted strangely with their faith in the protective power of the cow. They had, he claimed, such faith

The archer Arjuna obtaining a *Pashupatastra* or 'invincible weapon' from the God Shiva, on a carved panel from Chandimau in Bihar, 5th century. Now held at the Indian Museum, Kolkata, inv. NS2208-A25106.

in this animal that when they went to war, their cavalry took the hair of a wild ox and tied it to the necks of their horses, while infantrymen attached such hair to their shields or even tied it to their own hair.

Monuments to dead heroes remain common to many civilizations, but in India the *virakal* or *nadukal* 'memorial stone' developed in distinctive ways. The ancient practice of erecting standing stones over graves had largely been abandoned as cremation became almost universal. Carved memorials were only erected for recognized heroes and even this varied from state to state. For example, in 12th–14th-century Pandyan territory, hero stones were not only rarer than in neighbouring kingdoms but tended to be associated with major battles rather than individuals. Elsewhere, those located on the outskirts of villages presumably were intended to encourage villagers to defend their community in a time of frequent petty warfare.

According to Hindu religious texts, memorial stones which included a figural carving should face south, while those with a phallic lingam representing the god Shiva should face east or west. Other hero stones were erected within or next to temple complexes, or on the *ghats* (steps leading down to a body of water) where the bodies of the dead were cremated, or on the banks of rivers and lakes, on water-storage tanks, overlooking the coast, in the middle of forests, in foothills or simply in cemeteries. Religious texts gave instructions on the selection of suitable stone, how it should be purified under water and then rested on cereal grains for a specified time. The erection of the hero stone was then associated with rites including fire offerings and a *kumbhabhishekam* or consecration ceremony. In practice most hero stones were made from the hardest-available local stone or, if no such stone was available, from imported stone.

Stucco statuette of a warrior from Hadda in eastern Afghanistan, 5th or 6th century. Now held at the Musée Guimet, Paris.

Copper-plate texts issued by King Durvinita (r. 529–79) of the Western Ganja dynasty. Now held at the Government Museum, Bengaluru.

Petraglyph of a warrior or huntsman on a rock in the upper Indus valley of northern Pakistan, 5th–8th-century Buddhist period.

Hero stone from the reign of the Pallava king Simhavisnu (r. 575–600), 6th century, from Puliyanur, Dharmapouri.

One poem describing the respect given to a hero stone stated that people put peacock feathers on the image, along with wreaths made of *maral* flowers (the medicinal flower of the *Rhaponticum carthamoides* root). Another poem about a fallen hero proclaimed that when herds of cattle were stolen by the enemy, he not only won back the animals but caused such destruction amongst the foe that the owls gathered to feast upon the slain. The hero was nevertheless killed and as a result his wife was deprived of her lord, suffered widowhood and was bereft of all her jewels and beauty.

Indians had long been famed for their skill in astrology and the prediction of future events; this having a profound impact on warfare within medieval India, not least among the military caste. The 6th-century *Brihat Samhita* of Varahamihira, a widely respected book of astrology and auguries, included several chapters relating to military matters. One described ceremonies which a king should perform before going to war, included sitting on tiger skins, adorning himself, his elephants and horses with new white cloths, sandalwood paste (though in practice, henna was often used), perfumes and garlands. If a horse thus prepared and led to the king should stand with its left leg lifted from the ground the king would easily triumph, but if the horse became frightened, the king would suffer miseries. The priests should also give the horse a rice-ball and if the animal either smelled or ate the ball the king would triumph, but if not he would be defeated.

The *Brihat Samhita* stated that the astrological sign Vrishchika (Scorpio) represented horses and weapons, while meteors seen on any day other

FAR LEFT
Carving of Arjuna the archer standing next to Krishna, the eighth avatar of the God Vishnu, 5th- or 6th-century Gupta. Now held at the Museum für Asiatische Kunst, Berlin.

LEFT
Hero stone from Nellore in Andhra Pradesh, 7th-century Chola. Now held at the Government Museum, Chennai, acc. no. 117-39.

than that of a new or full moon could be a sign of war to come. If this phenomenon occurred when the sun was in the sign of Simha (Leo), merchants should store armour and weapons because there would be great profit in them; if in the sign of Kanya (Virgo) he should buy up asses, camels and horses then dispose of them in the sixth month when he would get double their value; if in the sign of Makara (Capricorn) he should buy up iron and other metals and sell at the end of the month. Another chapter focused on the marks which could be found on a sword, their precise positioning being indications of good or evil fortune. Furthermore, this astrological text insisted that a sword should not be taken out for no purpose, nor be rubbed against another substance, nor its edge looked at, nor its price stated, nor its place of manufacture mentioned, nor compared to anything else, nor touched by a person whom Hindu or more general Indian culture considered 'impure'.

After centuries of struggle and retreat, the later medieval period saw the emergence of a rather different bastion of Hindu power in the Vijayanagara kingdom of the deep south. This was not, however, merely a bastion of conservatism or simply a Hindu state which existed in defiance of Islamic pressure. Instead, Vijayanagara has been described as a successful late-medieval synthesis which incorporated aspects of the Indo-Islamic civilization of northern and central India. This was especially true of Vijayanagara's ruling, courtly and military elites, being evident in military technology, strategy, political and administrative structures, titles, terminology and material culture. Indeed, the historian Phillip B. Wagoner (1996) described it as a form of Islamization without conversion, while also noting that Islamic influence was more obvious in Vijayanagara's cavalry than its infantry.

Seated archer on an 8th-century terracotta plaque in the Somapura Mahavihara temple at Paharpur, Bangladesh.

Carved relief of Guardians of the Four Directions, from the Srimukhalingeswara temple in Mukhalingam, northern Andhra Pradesh, 8th century. Now held at the Government Museum, Chennai, acc. no. 84-14.38.

Hero stone from the reign of the Pallava king Nandivarman II (r. c.731–c.796) or Nandivarman III (r. c.846–c.869), 8th or 9th century, from Soirakulattur, North Arcot.

ELEPHANTS, HORSES AND CAMELS

The most striking aspect of warfare in medieval India was the importance of elephants which, together with cavalry, had replaced war chariots during the Gupta period. The few horse-drawn military vehicles which remained served as command-posts, while the bulk of baggage wagons were drawn by oxen.

Another feature of medieval India was its shortage of good quality warhorses, large numbers of which were constantly being imported across the mountains or by sea. This immediately raises the question of why, if ancient India had sufficient horses for large-scale chariot warfare, did medieval India lack sufficient cavalry mounts? Why was non-Islamic Indian cavalry considered less effective than that of its northern and western neighbours, and why did most non-Islamic medieval Indian states fail to field large numbers of mounted archers?

Horses were of course bred within India; the west of the country being considered best for this purpose while the east was better for elephants. Trade in both animals remained lucrative and a 13th-century inscription from the Pudukkottai district of Tamil Nadu actually listed taxes imposed on the trade in horses, elephants and iron. Other evidence shows that horse-dealers would gather from widely different regions at agreed places to trade with each other.

The differences between the generally larger and fiercer African elephant and the generally smaller and more docile Indian or Asian elephant are well known. In India, unlike China, local rulers took great interest in elephants as both practical and ritual animals. This was noted in the earliest Tibetan version of the 'Catalogue of the Kings of the Four Regions of the World', the second of whom was 'The King, who has in his power the science of the country of Magadha [ancient

Bihar], of the South and the Jewel of Elephants, the King of India' (Uray 1979: 296).

Despite persistent criticism by foreign military commentators, elephants were much more effective in battle than is generally thought – at least until the introduction of firearms. They were considered the most important military arm in non-Islamic medieval Indian military theory, and even in the *Ain-i-Akbari* ('Ritual of Akbar'), a detailed account of Mughul administration written for the Muslim Mughal Emperor Akbar (r. 1556–1605) in the 16th century, experienced men regarded a good war-elephant as worth 500 horses.

During the medieval period elephants were considered of no use until they were 15 years old, so they were normally captured from the wild rather than being bred in captivity. According to the *Arthashastra*, the process of capture began by encouraging a wild elephant to attach itself to a herd of already tamed elephants, after which the wild elephant was lured into a pit. The next stage was to keep this elephant confined within a particular area of forest rather than let it roam at large. According to 14th-century sources, a large number of workers and soldiers would enter the forest and build an extensive timber palisade with two openings, encircling an area which contained wild elephants. Some fierce but tamed war-elephants and their *mahouts* (drivers) were then sent into the palisade from one side while drummers entered noisily from the other. The trapped wild elephants then ran from side to side until, after a few days, they were exhausted. The *mahouts* now dismounted from their war-elephants and, apparently without too much difficulty, tamed the wild ones. Even more detailed information is found in the *Matanga-Lila* ('Elephant Sport') of Nilakantha, probably written in Kerala at a later date, which clearly drew upon long-established traditional lore.

The 7th-century writer Banabhatta was not alone in mentioning dummies made of leather that were used to train elephants in military manoeuvres, while the Persian traveller Abd al-Razzaq, sent to India as an ambassador by Shah Rukh (r. 1405–47) in 1442, stated that the training of captured elephants was done by two men in what might now be described as the 'good cop, bad cop' method. One man beat the well-chained elephant with a stick, after which the second man beat the first man, took away his stick and drove him off, this being repeated until the elephant came to regard the second man as his friend and was thus willing to be controlled by him.

Just over a century and a half later, the Italian traveller Ludovico di Varthema was clearly impressed by the war-elephants he saw on his visit, noting that a plank was placed between the boxes on the elephant's back, upon which the *mahout* sat and spoke to his mount. These impressive and expensive animals featured prominently during parades, a particularly vivid description being found in the *Harshacharita* ('Deeds of Harsha') by Banabhatta. This chronicler stated that some of the many elephants which came through the royal gate brought turbans of honour; others drums, some of which were new; while others were tributes or presents from other rulers or even the chiefs of 'wild tribes'. Some of the elephants appear to have been for use in mock battles. It was clearly an impressive spectacle, not only because of the size of these animals but also because they were abundantly decorated with banners, fine textiles, kettledrums, conch shells or cowrie shells, as well as having been sprinkled with perfumes.

Carving of Surya, the Sun God of Light and Daytime (above), and the subsidiary figure of a guardian (below), 9th-century Pala style from an unidentified site in Bihar. Now held at the Indian Museum, Kolkata, inv. 3933-A24144.

Hero stone from the reign of the first Chola king Vijayalaya Chola (r. *c.*850–*c.*870), 9th century, from Viracholapuram, South Arcot.

Hero stone from the reign of the Chola king Parantaka I (r. *c.*907–*c.*955), 10th-century Chola, from Talaiyuttu, North Arcot.

On campaign, war-elephants marched in the van of an army, could demolish defences and were even used to slow the flow of rivers, presumably by forming a sort of barrage downstream from where an army was to cross via boats, rafts or wading. Most medieval Islamic accounts of the Indians' use of war-elephants focused on how they could be defeated. The anonymous Persian romance *Iskandarnamah* ('Tale of Alexander'), however, written between the 12th and 14th centuries, gave a more balanced view of battle between Alexander the Great and the Indian king Porus (r. before 326–*c.*315 BC), who ruled part of the Punjab region. According to this Perso-Islamic version of Alexander's career of conquest, when the two armies came face to face, Porus ordered his *mahouts* to attack the enemy only if his other forces were defeated. Alexander's camel troops charged with incendiary weapons and archers, however, causing the elephants to flee. When Porus saw his elephants defeated, he reportedly admitted that it had been a mistake to hold back the great animals, and that he should have used them in his first assault.

Given the importance of elephants in Indian states and armies, it is not surprising that they were often highly decorated, sometimes with expensive items such as conch shells, especially on an elephant's ears, and cowrie shells, which were a traditional mark of status. Some locations seem, in fact, to have had a duty to supply their rulers with a limitless supply of seashells specifically for the adornment of elephants' ears.

All surviving pieces of elephant armour date from much later than the medieval period. Early written sources mention *varma* metallic armour, however, perhaps including mail, as well as large quivers to hold arrows, and even small *yantra* – a word normally taken to mean siege machinery. Some *Sukraniti* texts on the art of government referred to an elephant's body being protected by large pieces of armour resembling the leaves of wheat but made of iron, while the animal's trunk was protected by more flexible armour consisting of elements with sharp edges; probably scale or lamellar, but not mail.

Pictorial evidence for elephant armour is not always clear. For example, a brass incense burner of Jain origin from Gujarat, possibly made as early as the mid-6th century, is in the form of an elephant wearing a cloth caparison or armour. Even the clear representation of war- and parade elephants covered in large and highly decorated sheets shown in Hoysala art, might be interpreted as textile caparisons rather than armour.

A deep-seated Islamic prejudice against the use of elephants in war, or as demonstrations of royal power, would not prevent eastern Islamic and Indo-Islamic rulers for making considerable use of these impressive animals. Nevertheless, antipathy went back several decades before the dawn of the Islamic era and for many Muslims, elephants came to represent Satanic pride.

The *Chachnama* ('Story of the Chacha Dynasty'), which recounted the Arab-Islamic conquest of Sindh, though now believed to have been written in the 13th century, seems to have drawn upon earlier sources now lost. It also includes a great deal about Indian war-elephants. Thus, a letter reportedly sent by Muhammad Ibn Qasim to Raja Dahir son of Chach, the Hindu ruler in Sindh, asked the Raja why he took such pride in his elephants, then expressed the opinion that an elephant was

An elaborate 10th-century hero stone from Begur in Bengaluru. Now held at the Government Museum, Bengaluru.

devoid of intelligence and could not even defend its own body from a mosquito bite. It is unclear whether this text reflects Islamic attitudes of the 7th century, or of the 13th century.

Despite India's shortage of the best-quality cavalry mounts, the administrative system set up to register the characteristics and origins of horses, locally bred, imported or captured, dated back at least to the 3rd century. Imported horses enjoyed the highest status, but local breeds were also important. According to the Chinese visitor Xuanzang, in about 632 the Bamiyan area of eastern Afghanistan had abundant horses as well as cattle and sheep. Slightly further east, in what is now Pakistan, various medieval sources state that the finest local horses came from an area extending from Waziristan to Sindh. During the early-modern period, the best indigenous Indian horse for cavalry use was considered to be the Marwari breed, originating in the region of Marwar and existing for at least 1,000 years. The Marwari's most distinctive feature remains its ears, which can rotate 180 degrees and form a U-shape when curving towards the centre of its head. More significantly, perhaps, the breed was relatively resistant to disease.

Carved architectural relief showing a warrior, from an unidentified 10th-century location in Uttar Pradesh or Rajasthan. Now held at the Sackler Museum, Cambridge, MA, inv. 1961.134.

A warrior carved on the side of a 10th-century temple door, in Pala style from an unidentified location in Bihar. Now held at the Indian Museum, Kolkata, inv. UR60-A24207.

Detail from a multi-armed Bhairava manifestation of Shiva dating from about the 10th century, from West Dinajpur in West Bengal. Now held at the Indian Museum, Kolkata, inv. 72-2.

A high mortality rate among valuable imported horses during the medieval and later periods was widely attributed by foreign observers to an Indian ignorance of how to look after them. It is equally clear, however, that Indian stable masters knew very well how to look after native horses, so one may assume that local practices were simply unsuitable for the huge numbers of cavalry mounts brought to India overland and by sea.

Despite extremely uncomplimentary statements by later Muslim and European commentators, close attention had been paid to the training and care of horses in India from early times. According to the *Arthashastra*, for example, cavalry mounts were taught to carry out various movements in response to signals. Some of these movements were complex and did not come naturally to the horse. Several also sound remarkably similar to the *furusiyah* cavalry exercises developed in the medieval Islamic world.

Horse-furniture in India was influenced by a number of different traditions, both internal and external, but was also characterized by a prolonged survival of styles long after they were abandoned elsewhere. Even so, the Iranian scholar Abu Rayhan al-Biruni's assertion that early-11th-century Indians did not know of proper saddles, by which he probably meant saddles with wooden trees or frames, was clearly untrue among the military elite. Terracotta figures from as early as the 6th and 7th centuries, found in Uttar Pradesh and other parts of northern and north-western India, show saddles which are essentially the same as those used in Central Asia, China, Iran and the Middle East.

On the question of the adoption of stirrups in India, there are widely differing views. For example, while it is not true that stirrups spread to India during Ghaznavid Islamic conquests in the 10th and 11th centuries, the adoption of metallic stirrups was the result of influence from the north. One of the earliest clear written references to stirrups is in the *Manasollasa* ('Delight of the Mind'), a form of encyclopaedia written either by or for the Chalukya king Someshvara III (r. 1127–38) in about 1130. It mentions *padadharas* (stirrups) of gold hanging on both sides of a horse that was being made ready for a royal game of polo. Judging by medieval Indian carvings, substantial and often highly decorated leggings, chaps or boots were introduced around the same time.

The question of horse-armour is especially interesting in the Indian context, where a highly distinctive style appeared in the 12th-century Hoysala art of southern India. Contemporary depictions show cavalrymen with their legs thrust through holes in their horse-armour, presumably to grasp the horse because they were not using stirrups. The only other place where such a style was shown was, as far as the present author is aware, in immediately pre-Islamic Yemen. On the other hand, a 3rd-century Tamil poem called the *Mulaipattu* ('Forest [or 'Jasmine'] Song') does mention what is described as protecting shields for horses. Information drawn from Jain religious laws, codified in the 5th century, also mention warhorses with apparent armour. The situation becomes clearer in the 12th century, when the *Rajatarangini* ('River of Kings'), a chronicle of Kashmiri rulers, clearly mentions armoured horses.

Camels may have been used in desert areas of India such as Rajasthan from the 7th or 8th century onwards, immediately following the Muslim Arab conquest of neighbouring Sindh. Thereafter both the single-humped dromedary and the two-humped Bactrian camel were widely used for transport.

COMMUNICATIONS, TRADE AND TECHNOLOGY

India had a well-developed system of roads which not only crossed internal frontiers but were linked to longer-distance trade routes. These were of course used by armies as well as merchant caravans; some on the Indus–Ganges plain and along the northern edge of the Deccan retained strategic importance over millennia. The main north–south roads ran along the western side of peninsular India because the mountainous and forested interior made communications difficult. Nevertheless, the number of well-prepared roads was small and there were frequent references to armies having to cut their way through forest or bush, and having urgent need of local guides.

In earlier times some rulers were credited with planting fruit trees along major roads to provide food and shade for travellers, as well as having wells dug and rest-houses erected at regular intervals. Even in the less favoured medieval period, government officials in Hindu southern India were responsible for building and maintaining roads. Meanwhile, the precise distances given in Arab merchants' accounts of these trade routes were probably based upon an existing system of distance markers.

Most roads remained little more than unmade tracks, however, and were almost impassable during the rainy monsoon season. Unlike neighbouring Iran, medieval India built few large bridges. Instead major river crossings had state-regulated ferry services, while the *Arthashastra*

ABOVE & BELOW
The carved panels on the temple at Khajuraho in Madhya Pradesh are most famous for their erotic scenes, but those from the mid-10th or mid-11th century also show the pleasures of hunting at the time of the Chandela dynasty. Men on horseback and on foot are armed with a variety of weapons, including swords with angled rather than curved blades. (Frédéric Soltan & India Pictures via Getty Images)

Relief carving of Durga, the multi-armed Goddess of War, dating from the 10th- or 11th-century Chola period. Now held at the Puducherry Museum.

Carved panel showing an emanation of the Buddha attended by elephants, c.11th century from Madhya Pradesh. Now held at the Indian Museum, Kolkata, inv. NS2078-A24181.

advised rulers to ensure that rivers were only crossed at authorized places and times, supposedly to prevent 'traitors' escaping. Navigable rivers were also important highways for armies and merchant caravans but, despite a threat from river pirates, there is little evidence of real warfare on these waterways.

What is clear is that medieval India was not isolated from the wider world and al-Biruni's often-quoted statement that Hindus took no interest in foreign ideas has probably been taken too literally. While it may have been true of the priestly *brahmin* caste, it was clearly not true of the warrior and merchant castes. From at least the 13th century onwards, merchant guilds such as the southern Indian *Ayyavole* specialized in the *wootz* trade, these being small ingots of high-carbon crucible steel that were essential in the manufacture of high-quality weapons and armour. On the other hand, for several centuries medieval India was importing weapons and armour from the early Islamic world in exchange for largely plant-based goods such as food and textiles, plus high-value and exotic items including ivory and jewels.

Even before the expansion of Islam from the 7th century onwards, the hub of India's long-distance trade had shifted from the north to the south of the country, bringing increased wealth and power to southern Indian merchant castes and to southern rulers who could now afford bigger, better-equipped armies. This in turn led to the emergence of more powerful dynasties ruling more extensive territories. Northern India maintained its external links, of course, notably with Central Asia, Tibet and China. The remarkable story of medieval maritime links between India and China has rather overshadowed the overland links, where Assam served as the north-eastern Indian terminus. During the

ABOVE LEFT
Carving of Revanta the
Master of Horses, from an
unidentified location in the
Indian state of Bihar. Now held
at the Indian Museum, Kolkata,
inv. 3777-A24141.

ABOVE RIGHT
Carved relief of Veerabhadra, a
ferocious form of the god Shiva,
in 11th-century Chalukyan style.
Now held at the Government
Museum, Bengaluru.

8th century it is clear that Indian rulers from across northern India also sent emissaries seeking to strengthen diplomatic and military links. For example, the rulers of Kanauj in 736 and Kashmir in about 745 specifically asked for Chinese military aid to help fight against Tibetan aggression.

Trade with Central Asia resulted in slaves as well as merchants and soldiers moving across the massive mountain ranges which lay between. This had started at an early date and would increase through the medieval and early-modern centuries. In fact, large numbers of Hindus moved, willingly or otherwise, to Central Asia and during the early period they clearly included soldiers as well as skilled craftsmen and engineers. The evidence of documents, found in Central Asia and written in the language of what are now the North-West Frontier provinces of Pakistan, refers to a wide range of textiles and leather as well as seemingly complete articles of highly decorated costume, but rarely having a military association. The only exception seems to be the *kavasi,* which some scholars have linked with the Sanskrit words *kavacika, kavasa or kavaca,* which was perhaps a flexible form of armour. In contrast, trade links with Iran, Armenia and the Middle East included military items from an early date, an Indian sword being among other 'fine' instruments of war in the Persian *Kar-Namag-i Ardashir-i Babagan* ('Book of the Deeds of Ardashir, Son of Papak'), which probably dates from the late 6th or early 7th centuries.

Many letters written by Egyptian Jewish merchants survived in a hoard of documents from the Cairo Geniza. These confirm that iron and steel, traded as ingots rather than finished goods, were a major commodity shipped from India to Egypt, normally via Aden. Textiles are rarely mentioned in these documents and there is no mention of swords, whether Indian or otherwise. Of the items sent from Egypt via Aden to India, the largest number were textiles.

Knife with an ivory blade, perhaps for cutting paper and believed to be of medieval date, supposedly imported from India. Now held at the Museum of Islamic Art, Cairo, inv. 4180.

One of numerous carved panels illustrating episodes from the *Mahabharata* Hindu religious epic on the exterior of the Hoysaleswara Temple in Halebidu, in Karnataka, built between 1121 and 1160.

Study of ancient and medieval Indian technology has often focused on *wootz* steel and the Indian blades which were so renowned in the early Islamic world. Therefore it is surprising to find that iron working started later in India than in western Asia, while the associated techniques varied considerably within India. *Wootz* ingots were eventually made in the Middle East as well as India and were not 'super-steel' as was thought to be the case in the 19th and 20th centuries. Nor was *wootz* solely associated with arms and armour. In fact, excellent wire could be made from *wootz*, but for the manufacture of mail armour it had a reputation for being brittle.

Despite the lack of archaeological evidence for steel weapons in ancient India, a few high-carbon swords and axes have been found and there is no denying that *wootz* became a major theme in the writings of foreign commentators on India from the very early medieval period onwards. The reputation of Indian *wootz* then gradually declined in Arabic and Persian sources, however, with Indian steel no longer considered to be the best for sword-blades. In the early 11th century, al-Biruni noted that

(continued on page 33)

INDIA, 5TH TO 7TH CENTURIES
1: Alxon-Hunnic cavalryman, late 5th–6th centuries
2: Infantryman, Ganges plain, 5th–6th centuries
3: Infantry archer, central India, 5th–7th centuries
4: Infantryman, south of India, 6th–7th centuries

INDIA, 8TH & 9TH CENTURIES
1: Hindu-Shahi nobleman, 7th–8th centuries
2: War-elephant, northern India, 8th–9th centuries
3: Infantryman, Bengal or Orissa, 8th–9th centuries

INDIA, 10TH & 11TH CENTURIES
1: Gujarati cavalryman, 10th–11th centuries
2: Infantryman, 10th–11th centuries
3: Pratihara commander, 11th century

NORTHERN INDIA, 12TH & 13TH CENTURIES
1: Cavalryman, Kashmir, 12th–13th centuries
2: Infantry archer, north-western India, 12th–13th centuries
3: Kashmiri lady, 12th century

TRANSPORT, DECCAN & SOUTH, 12TH & 13TH CENTURIES
1: Gond tribal warrior, 12th century
2: Hoysa a war-elephant, 12th–13th centuries
3: Transport wagon, 12th–13th centuries

E

CAVALRY & INFANTRY, DECCAN & SOUTH, 12TH & 13TH CENTURIES
1: Hoysala cavalryman, mid-13th century
2: Eastern Ganga standard-bearer
3: Infantryman, south India

F

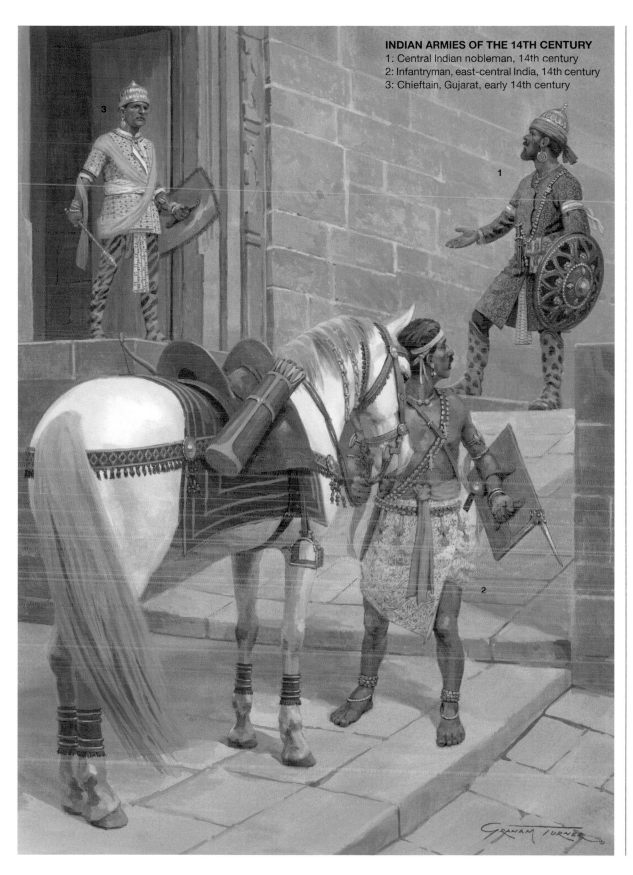

INDIAN ARMIES OF THE 14TH CENTURY
1: Central Indian nobleman, 14th century
2: Infantryman, east-central India, 14th century
3: Chieftain, Gujarat, early 14th century

INDIAN ARMIES OF THE 15TH CENTURY
1: Cavalryman, central India, mid-15th century
2: Hindu nobleman, south-central India, mid-15th century
3: Muslim mercenary, northern India, late 15th century

FAR LEFT
Carving of cavalrymen using a distinctive form of horse-armour previously seen in pre-Islamic Yemen; Kedareshwara Temple in Halebidu, dating between 1173 and 1220.

LEFT
An 11th–13th-century Indian leather shield on the ceiling of the rock-cut Biete Medhane Alem Church at Lalibela in Ethiopia.

small ingots of steel, known as 'eggs' and made in the Harat area of western Afghanistan, were being sent to India to be made into *sayf al-hind* – 'Indian swords' – while the Arab Muslim traveller al-Idrisi, writing in the 12th century, stated that Indian swordsmiths preferred iron from Sofala on the coast of what is now Mozambique in East Africa. A different perspective is provided by similarly dated Chinese sources, which state that *pin-t'ie* ('steel') was shipped to India from Sumatra and Java in what is now Indonesia.

Evidence for the prices and dues of goods arriving in Aden from the Malabar coast of south-western India include a merchant's letter from the year 1149. This remarkable surviving document mentions 20.4 *bahars* of iron valued at 17 *dinars* per *bahar*. At that time a *bahar* was probably between 100kg and 200kg, and this source was listing only one year's transactions between one pair of merchants, so the total volumes traded must have been much greater.

Almost a millennium and a half earlier, and on the other side of the Arabian Sea, the *Arthashastra* had much to say on weapons and the armouries in which they were stored. For example, it advised that the superintendent of the armoury should employ experienced workmen of tested ability to manufacture, in a given time and at fixed wages, wheels (probably meaning iron tyres for wagon wheels), weapons, armour and other accessory instruments for use in battle. All these weapons and instruments had to be kept in places which had been suitably prepared for them. Such military equipment was to be dusted frequently, moved from place to place and left in the sun for certain periods – perhaps to avoid rot. In fact, weapons likely to be affected by heat and damp or eaten by insects not only had to be kept in safe locations, but also had to be examined occasionally to assess their quality or condition, value and indeed quantities.

Like the merchants, certain craftsmen also formed their own guilds, despite or perhaps because of the fact that the social gap between skilled workers and those in charge of their industries increased during the first millennium. Metalworkers had a low status in the caste system and, like some other craft castes, were not allowed to beat drums, grow their hair long, hold high titles or own slaves. Nevertheless, some artisan guilds are known to have provided armed contingents to protect merchant caravans, at least until the middle of the 14th century.

ARMS AND ARMOUR

A significant number of weapons, and a much smaller number of items of armour, have been found in archaeological contexts in historic India. Those dating from the 3rd century BC to the 3rd century AD are generally similar to weaponry from neighbouring regions, and often reflect significant Iranian and Central Asian influence along with more surprising parallels with the Roman Mediterranean world.

Medieval Indian written sources are more generalized and not particularly helpful, merely referring to munitions being made in state arsenals. The terminology in such sources is also problematical as the precise meanings of many words remain unclear. Even the fact that Islamic rulers liked captured India blades and cuirasses merely states that these were of high quality, without further description. Other sources show that the sword was the most prestigious close-combat weapon, also having phallic symbolism and representing a man's martial prowess. It is also interesting to note that the *Brihat Samhita* identified a remarkable number of positive and negative omens and portents from small details of a sword, including its wear and tear.

Occasionally, commentators such as al-Mas'udi in the 10th century provide greater detail, stating that ivory was used in India for the hilts of daggers and for the guards of curved swords. Some swords in the *Arthashastra* had grips made of ivory, or the horn of rhinoceros or buffalo, though simpler wood or bamboo root were also mentioned. According to a detailed description of the sword of a young warrior, sent to the early-7th-century emperor Harsha (r. 606–47) from the Vindhya mountains by a tributary chieftain, his sword had either the tip of its blade or more probably its pommel silvered, a grip of polished horn and a wooden scabbard covered in spotted snakeskin, while the entire weapon was wrapped in black antelope skin.

During the early 13th century Fakhr-i Mudabbir (aka Fakhr al-Din Mubarakshah), a Persian Islamic scholar writing in northern India between 1157 and 1236, stated that Indian steel swords were sharper than others because they were made of purer metal. Fakhr-i Mudabbir also noted, however, that on the banks of the River Sindh, at a location identified as 'Kuraj' (perhaps Karachi), blacksmiths used two ingots of *wootz* to make a sword. The ingots were brought to the highest point of incandescence, with one twisted to the right and the other to the left; the sword was then encased in clay and deposited in a furnace for 24 hours before being forged, sharpened and polished to a shine. The method he describes is, of course, the pattern-welding method famously used in early-medieval Europe. Fakhr-i Mudabbir's reference to the shape of the point being like that of a persimmon leaf surely indicates that this sword-blade had the broadening and tapering leaf shape associated with the Indian *sosun pattah* ('lily leaf') short sword used by both Hindus and Muslims.

Spears and javelins were less prestigious weapons and were of course more common. The iconographic sources show weapons of very differing lengths, however, and it is often impossible to distinguish between thrusting spears and thrown javelins. Archaeological evidence from the medieval period is sparse when compared to the relative abundance of spear- and javelin-heads from the later centuries BC. Furthermore, the

ABOVE AND OPPOSITE
These iron short swords, excavated at Adichanallur in Tamil Nadu and now held at the Government Museum, Chennai, India, date perhaps from the late centuries BC to the earliest centuries AD.

known terminology is again difficult to interpret, though the *kasuari* is believed to have been a short lance, the *srka* a lance or a wooden shaft with metal spikes, and the *tomara* a long spear used from an elephant's back. The *Arthashastra* mentioned the *kunta* as a weapon with a blade like a ploughshare and a wooden haft 5–7 hand-spans long. Its name may be linked to the Romano-Greek *kontarion* and the Arabic *quntariya*. Traditional comments on javelins mentioned some which were very short, from only four hands' breadth long. In the 7th century Banabhatta stated that bundles of javelins were held in cases, while Xuanzang wrote that javelins were one of the chief weapons of Indian warriors. During the 12th, 13th and 14th centuries, Indo-Islamic writers confirmed the importance of such javelins, including the small but barbed *shil* often used from an elephant's back.

Infantry archery remained the primary arm in traditional Hindu Indian warfare, as well as having sacred connotations, and much information survives from early times concerning the weapons involved. Until the adoption of Turco-Persian-style composite bows, Indian bows were made of *tala* (*Borassus flabellifer Linn.* or the palmyra palm), *capa* (a type of bamboo), *daru* (an unidentified wood) and *srnga* (bone or horn). A type of bow called a *karmuka* was the most common, being made of *tala* wood, while the *kodanda* made of *capa* was regarded as sacred. Pictorial sources show simple curved or 'self' bows, however, often very long, as well as reflex bows in various shapes.

Indian 'self' bows varied in thickness as well as length, often being the height of a man. They were comparable to the so-called 'longbows' of medieval Europe and continued to be used by some hill tribes into modern times. In 1876, the British archaeologist and scholar M.J. Walhouse published an interesting account of such bamboo weapons being used by 'jungle tribe' hunters. He agreed with Fakhr-i Mudabbir that the bowstrings were made of rattan dried grass, while arrows of bamboo with large iron heads were shot from short range. These tribal archers did not draw their bowstrings to the ear, and barely to the breastbone, but nevertheless loosed their arrows with extraordinary force while holding the bow rather low. According to Walhouse, the arrow-shafts almost passed through the bodies of the animals which they struck.

Poisoned arrows were condemned in Hindu religious texts, but were nevertheless used. Fakhr-i Mudabbir was particularly concerned by such missiles, stating that the arrowheads used by those he referred to as mountain Indians largely consisted of bones poisoned with donkey urine and other filth. According to Fakhr al-Din such an arrow was called a *hadahani*.

Iconographical sources show infantry archers carrying quivers on their backs, sometimes two, while a hero might be described as looking as if he had four arms like a god, because of the quivers visible behind his shoulders. Other carvings show quivers fastened to the saddles of horses or to the backs of elephants. Usually cylindrical and sometimes highly decorated, they normally contained arrows with their heads pointing downwards.

The question of horse-archery is one of the most important in pre-modern Indian military history. This style of warfare was central to the success of most of the peoples whose migrations led them to establish states in India, Pakistan and Afghanistan. The decline of such states,

Some forms of Indian weapon persisted for more than 1,000 years, such as the large dagger or fighting knife with an all-metal H-shaped hilt. This example, in a private collection, is probably late medieval.

This knife was found buried in a stone circle between Kunur and Kartari in the Nigiri Hills in 1849; its present whereabouts are unknown.

however, which rarely lasted more than a few centuries, was almost invariably followed by a virtual abandonment of horse-archery. The Arabs and to a lesser extent Persians who built the first Islamic territories in what is now Pakistan did not make much of this tactic and it was not until a new wave of Turco-Islamic conquerors arrived that mounted archery became a major factor. Even then it seems to have been largely confined to Indo-Islamic armies and to Muslim mercenaries in Hindu or Jain employ.

Other weapons included the almost solely Indian *chakra* or *chakar* discus or sharp-edged quoit. It was an ancient idea but perhaps now become more sacred than practical. Lassos were also used, though more often by Central Asian invaders than by Indians themselves. The *gophana* or *gospana* sling had been widely used in ancient India and was still mentioned in 8th- and 9th-century Sanskrit texts. By that date, however, the word *gophana* also referred to the slings which formed part of stone-throwing siege weapons. Other medieval Indian weapons, perhaps used by forest and hill peoples, were the boomerang and the blowpipe. The former was described in the *Nitiprakasika* ('Expounder of Polity') – attributed to Vaisampayana, a pupil of the ancient Indian sage Vyasa who was himself credited with compiling the Hindi epic *Mahabharata* – as being two cubits long, having a knot at the foot and a long head, being one hand in breadth with its middle part bent outwards one cubit and with a sharp back. More practical, perhaps, were the curved throwing sticks used for hunting hare or small deer in southern India, but which did not return to the thrower. Blowpipes were used in a few places, primarily for hunting.

The dagger had special significance as a mark of status and masculinity in India, but its design tended to remain extremely traditional, with certain forms persisting for millennia. Once again, the written terminology poses problems; the *asi-putrika* being a short dagger attached to a girdle on the right hip or thigh and the *sasiri* being another short sword or dagger. The 9th-century *asidhenu*, or 'sister of the *asi*', was a fighting knife one cubit long and two thumbs wide but without a guard. Also from the 9th century was the thrusting *maustika* or *maustiku*, which was pointed and shaped like a small sword. As the personal weapon of rank-and-file infantry and soldiers on an elephant's back, it was one span long, with a pointed end, a high neck and a broad middle.

Most distinctive all was the Indian *katar* punch-dagger. With its horizontal grip and two extended flanges which went along the user's wrist and lower forearm, the *katar* appears in stone carvings in Orissa which might date from the 7th century, was certainly used and illustrated in 10th-century Orissa and, by the 13th century, was regarded by Fakhr-i Mudabbir as a primarily Hindu weapon.

It is possible that the long column-like mace carried by some rulers, heroes and divinities depicted in Indian art could be a symbolic 'churning stick' like those which allegorically churned a defeated enemy. More realistic, perhaps, were maces described in the *Sukraniti*, a book of advice for rulers, as having an octagonal head, being about 1.5m long with a strong handle.

The terminology of medieval Indian maces remains particularly problematical, however. For example, the *amukta* came in three forms, two of which were the *sthuna*, as tall as a man and covered in lumps,

Mounted archers occasionally appear in art from the Hoysala period, this example being on the Kedareshwara Temple in Halebidu, dating from between 1173 and 1220.

and the *gada*, which had an iron haft and 'one hundred spikes' on a large head two cubits long, the head and haft being equal length. The late-16th-century *Ausanasa Dhanurvea* book of Indian martial arts stated that the most suitable lengths were from 30 to 50 *anguli* (1.8–3m), the heavy heads demanding strength and stamina to wield. Though it could be spun around in the midst of enemy forces and was considered a very respectable weapon, it sounds more like something used in martial-arts or fitness training.

War-axes were also used in India. By the later medieval period they were probably much the same as those of the eastern Islamic countries in which a number of Indian forms appear to have been adopted at an early date. In fact, the widespread adoption of certain styles of war-axe may have been partly as a result of Indian influence spreading west rather than Iranian influence spreading east. Here it is interesting to recall the Sufi epic of Abu Muslim 'The Axe Bearer of Khurasan', which is known

Carving of an armoured horse at one corner of the star-shaped Chennakeshava Temple at Nagalapura, made in about 1200, showing the front of the caparison.

RIGHT AND BELOW
Memorial stone for Achaya-
sahani, chief of the camel-force
of Hoysala king Veera Ballala II
(r. c.1173–c.1220). Achaya was
killed in battle at Madevalli against
the Kalachuri king Sankamadeva
(r. 1177–80) between 1179 and
1184. Achaya is shown as a
camel-riding drummer shooting an
armour-wearing elephant driver
and an armoured cavalryman.
This hero stone was erected by
his widow and his son Mayideva.
Now held at the Archaeological
Museum, Halebidu, inv. 432,
Ins. No. Belur 339.

from at least the 12th century. It appears to be rooted in the Ghaznavid period and might reflect the military traditions of Indo-Iranian frontier warfare rather than Turkish Central Asian tradition. According to Fakhr-i Mudabbir's *Adab al-Harb wa'l-Shuja'ah*, the Indian *nachakh* was an axe with a half-moon blade and was considered a royal weapon.

One of the most striking aspects of the representation of warriors in medieval Indian art is their lack of armour and even helmets, despite the fact that various forms of such protection were mentioned in written sources. Indian archaeological evidence for helmets seems only available for the preceding centuries, though some pictorial and written sources suggest that medieval India shared forms of lamellar head protection with several neighbouring areas.

LEFT AND BELOW
This particularly fine hero stone
portraying two equally matched
and armoured warriors records
the death of Dasadeva, a member
of a powerful aristocratic family.
He was credited with saving the
day during a desperate battle
against rebels under Bijjanadeva,
but was killed in the process.
The hero stone was set up by his
widow Sanatavve and its date
corresponds to 19 April 1220,
at the start of the reign of the
Hoysala king Vira Narasimha II
(r. 1220–34). Now held at the
Archaeological Museum, Halebidu,
inv. 567, Ins. No. Belur 332.

A recently discovered helmet with a magnificent pagoda-shaped finial
or crest (currently in private hands) appears to be associated with the
Saffarid dynasty of Afghanistan and eastern Iran, and to date from the
10th century. It was probably manufactured in Ghur and could be taken as
evidence that one-piece steel helmets remained widespread across these
regions – including northern India – from the earliest Islamic centuries.

Written sources, both Indian and Islamic, add further details. For
example, al-Tabari's reference to a mixed Tibetan, Turk and *Hayatilah*
(Hephthalite) attack on Arab-held Tirmidh (Termez) in 704, recorded
that the attackers suffered high losses among those with crested
helmets and even more among those with smooth helmets. The former
were either a military elite or were from a group who distinguished
themselves by wearing helmets with distinctive crests – perhaps like the

Seal attached to a copper-plate grant of the Yadava ruler Krishna (Kannara), dated 1171 of the Shaka era (1249).

Despite their late date of 1258, many of the exterior carvings on the Chennakesava Temple at Somanathapura in Karnataka, are quite crude and may never have been finished.

'pagoda-shaped' crest mentioned above. Early Indian written sources provide terminology which is particularly difficult to interpret in the absence of pictorial sources. For example, Kautilya and others list head protections such as the *sirastrana* (cover for the head) and *kanthatrana* (cover for the neck), with the former probably ranging from a steel helmet to a thickly wound turban. Far away in late-9th-century Spain, Islamic al-Andalus imported Indian helmets made of wood, according to the Persian geographer Ibn Khurdadhbih. Unfortunately, most 11th-, 12th- and 13th-century representations of Indian warriors show them bareheaded. A sort of flat-topped head-covering is shown in 12th–13th-century Hoysala south Indian carvings but, being unlike anything else, this is more likely to show a form of turban. Indeed, most pictorial and written sources suggest that thickly wound turbans were considered a sufficient protection in India's hot climate.

Indian armour from this period was undoubtedly light, where worn at all, and remained so until the late-medieval period. Mail was shown in Buddhist art from pre-Islamic eastern Afghanistan and, less clearly, in a 12th-century wall-painting in Ladakh. A handful of Hoysala carvings from late-12th- or 13th-century Karnataka show a form of sometimes decorated breast-protection, on one occasion with upper-arm protection. References to armour in Indian documentary sources are, however, both varied and difficult to interpret or to associate with the limited pictorial evidence. Ancient *Vayu Purana* Hindu religious texts made it clear that neither *kavacha* nor *drapi* types of armour were arrow-proof, despite the fact that the *kavacha* was also described as an 'iron coat' with separate pieces for the chest, back, head, trunk and arms.

Other early-medieval sources list further forms, including the *kurpasa* covering for the chest and abdomen, and the *kanchuka* coat extending to hands or knees mentioned in the *Amarakosha* (4th–7th centuries) as a body armour. In the 7th century a description by Banabhatta of the

kanchuka worn by chieftains stated that it was a tunic-shaped garment. The *Amarakosha* also includes the *varavana* or *varabana* as body armour and elsewhere this was said to be an 'arrow proof' coat reaching the heels. The term *pattah* was also used for an 'iron leaf coat' which lacked protection for the arms while the large *lohajala* included a coif to protect the head, which the smaller *lohajalika* did not. Both were hauberks of 'iron net' and thus almost certainly of mail, while *nagodarika* were protective mittens. The *sutraka* or *sutra-kankata* protected only the abdomen and hips and was almost certainly a quilted cotton soft armour.

Medieval India was clearly not a major centre of armour production. For example, the 9th-century 'Examination of Commerce', wrongly attributed to al-Jahiz, omits anything military in its list of Iraq's imports from India. In contrast, the frontier region of Ghur in present-day Afghanistan was a major source of lamellar *jawshan* cuirasses while Tibetan cuirasses were also highly regarded.

Surviving Indian armours all date from well after the medieval period, but nevertheless include protections which are lined, internally or externally, with scales of various materials including those of the pangolin or scaly anteater. Meanwhile, the earliest surviving quilted armour from Central India and Rajasthan is similar to examples from Central Asia. The famous Indian 'coat of a thousand nails' was a quilted armour in which the padding and, when present, a layer of scales were secured by numerous rivets. It probably evolved from earlier quilted and scale armour.

Medieval Indian shields were notably varied, ranging from the tasselled lower D-shaped shield on an ivory of warriors from Patna to the oblong shields of rock-carved door guards at Pitalkhora which were similarly decorated with tassels plus small bells. Some recently discovered medieval Indian leather shields in a rock-cut church at Lalibela in Ethiopia include one the exterior of which is decorated with mother-of-pearl and another the interior of which has a painting of warriors or hunters. The quality of Indian leather shields was such that they were held in high regard until the 19th century, by which time many were habitually decorated with gilded bosses and pattern of silver leaf.

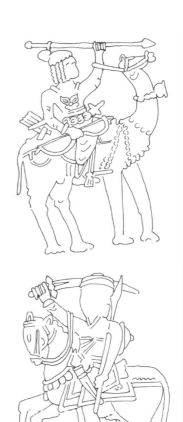

Hero stones from Sindh: above, a camel-riding warrior of the Rabari people in Sabusan village, Nagarparkar, in south-eastern Sindh, Rajput, probably 13th or 14th century; below, defaced hero stone of a horseman in Khanpur village, Nagarparkar, probably 14th or 15th century.

In contrast to some finely carved earlier hero stones, this 15th-century example from the village of Maragallu, in the Kolara district of Karnataka, is in a very simple style. Now held at the Government Museum, Bengaluru.

Bronze statuette of the saintly archer Kannappa Nayanar dating from the 15th century, from the Tirivallore district of Tamil Nadu. Now held at the Government Museum, Chennai, acc. no. 338.

A 15th-century copy of the works of Jain monk Kalakacharya, dating from the late 3rd–early 2nd centuries BC.

Returning to the earlier centuries, Kautilya's *Arthashastra* listed shields of several kinds: the *veti* made of 'interwoven creeper' which may have been a large mantlet or a smaller spiral shield; the widely used leather *charma*; the *hastikarma* described as a board to cover the body and shaped like an elephant's ear (perhaps D-shaped); the *talamula* supposedly capable of driving back elephants; the *la* or simple wooden shield; the seemingly 'trumpet-shaped' *dhamanika* which was probably very convex in form; the 'door-shaped' wooden *kavata*; the *kitika* of leather or bamboo bark; the *apratihata* to protect against elephants; and the *valahakanta apratihata*, which was similar but with a spiked metal rim.

According to Banabhatta in the 7th century, *karda-ranga* leather or rawhide shields were used across most of the country; and in the 11th century al-Biruni noted that the eight guilds with whom no other people would intermarry included the basket and shield makers, surely indicating that the shields in question were woven like basketwork. Just under a century earlier al-Mas'udi had written that the shields of Hind and Sind were not the same as those of Zanj (the medieval Arabic term for east Africa). The latter, like those of the Indians, included *daraqa* shields made of elephant hide but were nevertheless not as strong as the *daraqa* shields of China, Tibet and the Beja people of north-eastern Sudan.

Where incendiaries are concerned, early and traditional Indian sources can be especially misleading. Nevertheless, such weapons were highly developed in ancient and medieval India. For example, the ancient *agneya-stras* were recipes for varied, sometimes strange but clearly flammable mixtures, though most of the ingredients mentioned in the *Arthashastra* were vegetable rather than petroleum based. One source, however, almost certainly does refer to a petroleum-based incendiary. This was a Sanskrit poem by Bilhana, written in the last quarter of the 11th century and describing the love-smitten Western Chalukya King Vikramaditya VI (r. 1076–1126) before his marriage to Queen Chandala Devi. The poet wrote that the God of love produced in his arrows shot at the king the fire lit from *Parasika* (Persian) oil, the intense heat of which could not be quenched either by icy water or by liquids made of sandalwood paste. A commentary on this poem, dating to about 1286, explained that it referred to fire lit with oil produced in the Parasika country – present-day Iran.

Suggestions that cannon were used in India by both Hindus and Muslims in the mid-13th century are a misinterpretation of the term 'western stone throwers'. The weapons in question were actually trebuchets, described as *Maghribi* or 'western' because they were of originally North African or European design. Nevertheless, the pyrotechnics or incendiaries used in the Vijayanagara kingdom of southern India, as recorded in 1443 by the Persian ambassador Abd al-Razzaq, almost certainly did include gunpowder. Somewhat over a generation later – according to the *Ras Mala*, a collection of chronicles and traditional histories collected by the British colonial administrator Alexander Kinlock Forbes in the mid-19th century – hand-gunner musketeers and cannon were employed by Sultan Mahmud Begada of Gujarat (r. 1458–1511) against the pirates of Bulsar in 1482. Late-15th-century Gujarat maintained close relations with the Mamluk Sultanate of Egypt from where such weapons and their gunners were probably enlisted, both states having an interest in driving pirates from the sea-lanes of the Arabian Sea.

FURTHER READING

Afif, S.S., trans. R.C. Jauhri (2001). *Medieval India in Transition: Tarikh-i-Firoz Shahi, A First Hand Account*. New Delhi: Sundeep Prakashan.

Agarwala, V.S. (1951). 'An Old Reference to Persian Oil in Sanskrit Literature', *Proceedings and Transactions of All-India Oriental Conference, Thirteenth Session: Nagpur University October 1946* (Nagpur): 63.

Ahmed, M. (2012). 'The Long Thirteenth Century of the Chachnama', *The Indian Economic and Social History Review* 49: 45–91.

Aiyangar, S.K. (1921). *South India and her Muhammadan Invaders*. Oxford: Oxford University Press.

Aiyangar, S.K. (1931). *Evolution of Hindu Administrative Institutions in South India*. Madras: University of Madras.

Altekar, A.S. (1949). *State and Government in Ancient India, from earliest times to c.1200 A.D.* Banaras: Motilal Banarsidass.

Anon., trans. M.S. Southgate (1978). *Iskandarnamah: A Persian Medieval Alexander Romance*. New York, NY: Columbia University Press.

Anooshahr, A. (2018). 'The Elephant and the Sovereign: India circa 1000 CE', *Journal of the Royal Asiatic Society* 3.28: 615–44.

Banabhatta, ed. P.V. Kane (1965). *The Harshacarita of Banabhatta (Text of Ucchvasas I–VIII)*. Delhi: Motilal Banarsidass.

Bhakari, S.K. (1981). *Indian Warfare: An Appraisal of Strategy and Tactics of War in early medieval period*. New Delhi: Munshiram Manoharlal.

Bronson, B. (1986). 'The Making and Selling of Wootz, a Crucible Steel of India', *Archeomaterials* 1: 13–51.

Chakhravarti, P.C. (c.1941). *The Art of War in Ancient India*. Dacca: Ramna.

Chandra, M. (1960). 'Indian Costumes and Textiles from the Eighth to the Twelfth Century', *Journal of Indian Textile History* 2: 1–41.

Deloche, J. (1986). *Le Cheval et son harnachement dans l'Art Indien*. Lausanne: Caracole [Ecole française d'Extrême Orient].

Deloche, J. (1989). *Military Technology in Hoysala Sculpture (Twelfth and Thirteenth Century)*. New Delhi: Sitaram Bhartia Institute of Scientific Research.

Digby, S. (1971). *War-Horse and Elephant in the Delhi Sultanate: A Study of Military Supplies*. Oxford: Orient Monographs.

Digby, S. (1996). 'The Arabian and Gulf horse in medieval India', in D. Alexander, ed., *Furusiyya, vol. 1: The Horse in the Art of the Near East*. Riyadh: The King Abdulaziz Public Library: 162–67.

Edgerton, F. (1931). *The Elephant-Lore of the Hindus: The Elephant-Sport (Matanga-lila) of Nilakantha*. New Haven, CT: Yale University Press.

Elgood, R. (2004). *Hindu Arms and Ritual: Arms and Armour from India 1400–1865*. Delft: Eburon Academic.

Fakhr al-Din Mubarakshah, Muhammad Ibn Mansur [Fakhr-i Mudabbir], ed. A.S. Khwansari (1969). *Adab al-Harb wa'l Shuja'ah*. Tehran: Intisharat-i Iqbal.

Fakhr-i Mudabbir [as Sharif Muhammad Mansur Mubarakshah], trans. S.N. Babadzhanov, et al. (1997). *Adab al-kharb va-sh-shudzhaat (Pravila voinyi muzhestvo)*. Dustanbe: Tadzhikskii Vysshii Voennyi Kolledzh. Russian translation of Persian text.

Forbes, A.K. (1865). *Ras Mala, Hindoo Annals of the Province of Goozerat in Western India*. London: Richardson Brothers.

Govindasami, S.K. (1939). 'The Army of the Later Cholas (900–1200)', *Journal of the Bombay Historical Society* 5: 101–18.

Kalhana, trans. M.S. Stein (1900). *Kalhana's Rajatarangini: A Chronicle of the Kings of Kasmir*. London: Constable & Co.

Kautilya, trans. R. Shamasastry (1923). *Kautilya's Arthashastra*. Mysore: Wesleyan Mission Press.

Kennedy, R.S. (1976). 'The King in Early South India, as Chieftain and Emperor', *The Indian Historical Review* 3: 1–15.

Majumdar, B.K. (1955). *The Military System in Ancient India*. Calcutta: World Press.

Mas'udi, Abu'l-Hasan Ali In al-Husain al-, ed. & trans. C. Barbier de Maynard & Pavet de Courteille (1861–77). *Muruj al Dahab – Les Prairies d'Or*. Paris: Imprimerie Impériale.

Narayanan, M.G.S. (1973). 'The Institution of "Companions of Honour" with Special Reference to South India', in T.K. Ravidran, ed., *Journal of Indian History Golden Jubilee Volume*. Kerala: Department of History, University of Kerala: 181–92.

Nicolle, D. (2019). 'Helmets or Hard-Hats? Some Wood-lined Headgear from Mamluk Syria', in M. Eychenne, S. Pradines & A. Zouache, eds, *Guerre et paix dans le Proche-Orient Médiéval (Xe–XVe siècle)*. Cairo: Institut français d'archéologie orientale du Caire: 115–27.

Nilakanta Sastri, K.A. (1939). *Foreign Notices of South India from Megasthenes to Ma Huan*. Madras: University of Madras.

Nordlunde, K. (2013). 'How Old is the Katar?', *Arms & Armour: Journal of the Royal Armouries* 10: 71–80.

Prakash, B. (1962). 'Some Aspects of Indian Culture on the Eve of Muslim Invasions', *The Research Bulletin (Arts) of the University of the Panjab* 39: 1–117.

Rawson, P.S. (1968). *The Indian Sword*. London: Herbert Jenkins.

Robinson, H.R. (1967). *Oriental Armour*. London: Herbert Jenkins.

Srivastava, A.L. (1965). 'A Survey of India's Resistance to Medieval Invaders from the North-West: Causes of Eventual Hindu Defeat', *Journal of Indian History* 43: 349–68.

Uray, G. (1979). 'The Old Tibetan Sources of the History of Central Asia up to 751 A.D.: A Survey', in J. Harmatta (ed.), *Prolegomena to the Sources on the History of Pre-Islamic Central Asia*. Budapest: Akadémiai Kiadó: 275–304.

Vaidyanathan, K.S. (1947–48). 'Hero Stones', *The Quarterly Journal of the Mythic Society* 38: 128–38.

Varahamihira, trans. N. Chidambaran Iyer (1884). *The Brihat Samhita of Varaha Mihira*. Madura: South Indian Press.

Wagoner, P.B. (1996). '"Sultan among Hindu Kings": Dress, Title and Islamization of Hindu Culture in Vijayanagara', *Journal of Asian Studies* 55: 851–80.

Walhouse, M.J. (1876). 'Indian Arrow-Heads', *The Indian Antiquary* 5: 362.

Yadava, B.N.S. (1973). *Society and Culture in Northern India in the Twelfth Century*. Allahabad: Central Book Depot. Reprinted (2001) as 'Chivalry and Warfare', in J.J.L. Gommans & D.H.A. Kolff, eds, *Warfare and Weaponry in South Asia 1000–1800*. Oxford: Oxford University Press: 66–98.

PLATE COMMENTARIES

A: INDIA, 5TH TO 7TH CENTURIES

(1) Alxon-Hunnic cavalryman, late 5th–6th centuries

During the early-medieval period, military equipment in what are now north-western Pakistan and eastern Afghanistan reflected a variety of influences, primarily from India but also from Iran and Central Asia. This area also has its own military-technological traditions, which would include this horseman's one-piece round helmet whereas his limited form of mail shirt is perhaps more Iranian. The method of hanging his sword was also originally Iranian, but by this period it had been adopted across a large part of Asia, including much of India. One of the few aspects of his equipment which might be identified as Hunnic is the long-hilted sword with its simple bar guard inlaid with semi-precious stones. His jewellery and the decorations on his belts reflect close cultural links with India. The most notable features of his horse-harness are a lack of stirrups, the low saddle, the trimmed mane and the bronze curb-bit which forms an integral part of the bronze caveson nose-band.

(2) Infantryman from the Ganges plain, 5th–6th centuries

A number of foreign military features persisted in northern and central India until the middle of the first millennium, but would then disappear. They appear to have included a coat with extravagantly long sleeves and a fluted head-covering that is sometimes interpreted as a helmet but was more likely to have been a thickly quilted cap. This foot soldier's only other protection is a substantial rectangular shield which, judging by written sources, may have been made of interwoven reeds, perhaps bound with strips of leather. He is armed with a dagger and spear for close combat, plus two bamboo-hafted javelins, one of which has a blade with four edges set at right angles to each other. His long, loose-fitting linen leggings, held up by unseen laces, were probably of Parthian origin and seem to have been a fashion which lasted longer in India than elsewhere. In fact, the only part of his attire which was specifically Indian is the *dhoti*, a long and broad rectangular piece of cloth wound around the waist and under the crotch. Of ancient origin and very suitable for the Indian climate, the *dhoti* would persist until modern times.

(3) Infantry archer from central India, 5th–7th centuries

Medieval Indian art shows the great majority of warriors entirely unarmoured. They usually wear a *dhoti* though a significant number in central and southern India only wear a form of loincloth wound in a similar way. Another distinctive feature of traditional Indian male appearance was very long hair, especially among the *brahmin* priestly and *kshatriya* noble or warrior castes. The man's abundant jewellery is also typical of the *kshatriya*. In terms of military equipment, this infantry archer is notable for his simple but very long wooden bow with its bowstring of rattan, and the way he straps a quiver on his back with ribbons around his abdomen and over one shoulder.

(4) Infantryman from the deep south of India, 6th–7th centuries

An unexpected item of warrior clothing shown in early-medieval Indian art was a sort of close-fitting T-shirt, probably of cotton, which covered the shoulders and chest but not the midriff. It was worn with a normal *dhoti*. In addition to a shield of interlaced cane with a simple wooden grip, this man is armed with a heavy reverse-curved sword. Used across much of the subcontinent, this weapon would remain characteristic, especially of southern Indian warriors, throughout the medieval period. It may also have been the prototype of later weapons such as the Gurkha *kukri* and the Afghan *peshkabz* or 'Khyber Knife'.

B: INDIA, 8TH AND 9TH CENTURIES

(1) Hindu-Shahi nobleman, 7th–8th centuries

As the armies of the early Islamic conquests swept east, they were fought to a standstill in eastern Afghanistan and northern Pakistan by the Hindu-Shahi realm. This militarily successful state is here represented by a member of its notably well-equipped military aristocracy. His splinted iron helmet incorporates laminated cheek-pieces and is of a style found across much of Central Asia and neighbouring territories. The garment over his short-sleeved, mid-length mail hauberk appears to have been quilted. In addition to a fighting knife hung horizontally in Turco-Iranian style, he is armed with a straight sword with a notably long hilt. There is also a fluted mace thrust beneath his fully framed form of saddle. The curb-bit incorporates a metal caveson which would press down on the horse's nose, inhibiting its breathing, when the rider pulled the reins.

(2) War-elephant from northern India, 8th–9th centuries

According to written sources, a surprising number of warriors could ride on a single elephant, but here the number has been reduced to three: the *mahout* or driver, a nobleman or commander, and a javelin thrower. Some war-elephants were already armoured, though the majority were not. The howdah on the animal's back could also vary; this example being primarily based upon an ivory figurine dating from the 8th–10th centuries. The wooden structure offers little protection, with the unarmoured *mahout* and javelin thrower clinging to it being particularly exposed. The basic elephant harness would remain largely unchanged from ancient to early-modern times. The senior man sitting on cushions inside the howdah wears a decorated small cape, seemingly associated with Buddhist rather than Hindu culture. His *dhoti* was, however, a long-established Indian male garment which could be wound in a number of different ways. His dagger is also typically Indian, as is the method of strapping two quivers on his back. Despite being recurved, his bow is of wooden rather than composite construction. Armour, though occasionally mentioned in written sources, was only rarely depicted in early Indian art. The javelin thrower's large quilted cap probably had a protective function, however, and may have reflected the influence of earlier invading peoples. In other respects, he is typically Indian in relying only upon a shield for protection. For offensive purposes he is armed with short-hafted javelins, suitable for use from the back of an elephant. The skilled *mahout* who controls the elephant is not only unarmed and unprotected but is virtually naked, wearing only a brief loincloth plus a cloth across his chest which might be a blanket to throw around his shoulders at night. The object with a blunt pike and a curved hook is his *ankusha*, a device to communicate commands to the elephant by prodding its neck or pulling its ears.

(3) Infantryman from Bengal or Orissa, 8th–9th centuries

Yet again an infantry warrior, though wealthy enough to wear abundant jewellery and a richly decorated *paridhana* cloth belt multiple times around his hips, and to possess a good-quality sword and a substantial rhinoceros-hide shield, scorns any armour. This was probably for cultural and climatic reasons. His straight, double-edged sword is of a typical early-medieval Indian form which had long been held in high esteem in the Arabian Peninsula.

C: INDIA, 10TH AND 11TH CENTURIES

(1) Gujarati cavalryman, 10th–11th centuries

From the 8th century to the 14th century, a number of military fashions that were falling out of fashion in the Islamic lands, persisted in India for hundreds of years. Although Indian military technology and systems had some limited influence in neighbouring Islamic territories, the flow of influence was mostly in the opposite direction. For example, this rider's costume and equipment are typically Indian, especially his lack of armour despite riding an armoured horse, whereas his riding boots, the hanging of his scabbard and above all his horse's quilted horse-armour are in a pre- or early Islamic Iranian style. The metal-framed caveson bridle seems to take an Iranian concept even further than it was in early eastern Islamic lands. The horse itself is an indigenous breed, the Marwari with its distinctive inward-curving ears.

(2) Infantryman from south-central India, 10th–11th centuries

In ancient and medieval India, highly decorated parasols served as standards and rallying points for armies, as well as being marks of royalty. Those who carried them in battle naturally formed an elite, and were abundantly decorated themselves. This parasol-bearer's rectangular shield has two cow's tails fastened to the front; these were believed to provide almost sacred protection. Also note his distinctive single-edged, slightly reverse-curved sword which is within a tradition that later included the *kukri* short-sword or large fighting knife of Gurkha soldiers.

(3) Pratihara commander, 11th century

Today the turban is widely regarded as a traditional Islamic form of head-covering, but in fact it was copied by early-medieval Islamic peoples from their Indian neighbours, though initially in Afghanistan rather than India itself. The pre-Islamic civilizations of much of northern India had long been under military and cultural influence from Iran and Central Asia, largely as a result of repeated invasions. Consequently, this high-status officer from the Pratihara kingdom reflects both local and external influences, from his turban and abundance of jewellery, to his silver- and gold-decorated helmet which nevertheless basically consists of a strong steel headpiece. His mail shirt is in an Iranian style whereas his leggings and boots look Central Asian and his bronze elephant-headed war-hammer is distinctively Indian, as is the enthusiastic use of sandalwood paste to colour his horse's tail, mane, forelock, nose and fetlocks.

D: NORTHERN INDIA, 12TH AND 13TH CENTURIES

(1) Armoured cavalryman from Kashmir, 12th–13th centuries

Indian pictorial sources, ranging from Buddhist monastery wall-paintings in Ladakh to Hindu and Jain temple or memorial carvings in Karnataka, show that there were periods when armour was more widely worn in India. Nevertheless, the majority of Indian warriors clung to their traditional reliance upon shields to protect their bodies in a climate where the wearing of armour was exhausting and sometimes

Carving of a bare-chested warrior with a saddle-sword beneath his thigh on the mid-13th-century Chennakesava Temple at Somanathapura in Karnataka.

impossible. In fact, the portrayal of full Turco-Mongol lamellar armour, as worn by this Kashmiri, probably reflected a passing fashion inspired by recently arrived invaders, mercenaries, allies or neighbours. His helmet is based upon a decorated ceremonial crown from neighbouring Nepal that itself seemed to be based upon a form of helmet. His sword and shield are entirely Indian in style, as is the abundant decoration of his horse.

(2) Armoured infantry archer from north-western India, 12th–13th centuries

This infantryman is based upon a remarkable wall-painting in a Buddhist monastery in Ladakh. Several aspects of his equipment either reflect a tradition rarely seen elsewhere in India, or the influence of a militarily significant neighbour, in this case almost certainly from the eastern provinces of the Islamic world. Thus, his quilted, cloth-covered but sleeveless 'soft armour' and his mail-lined, padded coif are eastern Islamic in style, though the man's long hair pulled through the laced rear opening is distinctly Indian. His massive wooden bow and simple wooden shield could have been shared by infantry soldiers across a great many countries, even to some extent in southern India, which in other respects had a very different military culture.

(3) Kashmiri lady, 12th century

The differences between the costume of the female elites of northern and southern India, as portrayed in Buddhist, Hindu and Jain art, seem to have been at least as great as the differences in traditional male costume. Climatic and other factors probably played a significant role, this woman again being largely based upon wall-paintings in the Buddhist monasteries at Alchi in Ladakh, where local traditions had much in common with neighbouring Tibet to the east and Islamic Central Asia to the north. She is being conveyed in a *palki* or palanquin carried by two bearers.

E: TRANSPORT OF THE DECCAN AND SOUTH, 12TH AND 13TH CENTURIES

(1) Gond tribal warrior, 12th century

Significant numbers of tribal warriors served in the armies of more settled states, while the Gond of central India also formed their own Chanda state at the beginning of the 13th century. Their art illustrates warriors who are equipped in a similar manner to other south Indian military forces. His reverse-curved, single-edged sword appears to be an exaggerated version of a style of weapon used across much of the subcontinent, but the substantial nose-ring worn by this man may be a tribal fashion. In this reconstruction the Gond warrior is employed as a humble 'bearer', using a shoulder-pole to carry two ceramic pots of drinking water.

(2) Hoysala armoured war-elephant, 12th–13th centuries
This fully armoured war-elephant, its howdah, and its crew are based upon a mid- to late-13th-century memorial stone that commemorates the heroic actions of a member of the Hoysala army. The decorated rings around the elephant's tusks would help stop these splitting in violent combat while the wooden 'castle' has an almost cross-shaped plan. This probably reflected the positioning of the covered supporting frame on the elephant's back, while the animal's armour consists of decorative cloth over protective quilted elements. On this occasion the *mahout* has a limited form of thickly quilted and brightly embroidered 'soft armour', though only over his chest, perhaps including a layer of leather or metallic elements. He also has a substantial broad-bladed dagger, while his abundant jewellery, printed cotton *dhoti* and brightly coloured *paridhana* textile belt under a sash probably reflect the status of the man in the howdah rather than that of the *mahout* himself. Unlike his *mahout*, the commanding officer does not wear armour, perhaps reflecting the fact that in southern Indian culture the wearing of such protections was seen as a fundamentally undesirable necessity rather than a mark of status. It is also worth noting that, despite this relatively late date, the man still carries an archaic but also almost sacred bamboo bow. The carrying of a quiver on his back was similarly archaic, though clearly still practical.

(3) Two-wheeled transport wagon, 12th–13th centuries
The slow speed at which traditional Indian armies moved was noted by their opponents throughout the medieval and early-modern periods. This was the result of geography and climate, the condition of the roads and the sheer size of the forces involved. While different pack animals were also used, the primary method of moving supplies remained the slow-moving ox-cart, here drawn by a pair of *zebu* humped Indian oxen. The continued use of solid wheels, in this case with iron tyres, may have reflected the rough terrain to be covered. The wagon driver is portrayed as a Hindu ascetic wearing a *kaupinam* or minimal loincloth with a begging bowl around his neck. Whether a pious ascetic would deign to protect himself from the rains with a shepherd's cloak is open to question.

F: CAVALRY AND INFANTRY OF THE DECCAN AND SOUTH, 12TH AND 13TH CENTURIES
(1) Hoysala armoured cavalryman, mid-13th century
The sudden appearance of body armour on 13th-century Hoysala memorial or hero stones in the Karnataka region, and more rarely in Hoysala temple carvings, is yet to be explained. It likely reflected the fact, however, that this part of India, previously barely impacted by Islamic invasions, now found itself on the front line facing Islamic foes whose military technology was generally more advanced than that of the Hoysala kingdom itself. The carvings upon which this figure's cuirass is based have therefore been interpreted in terms of what is known about similar 12th–14th-century eastern Islamic scale-lined armours. His double-ended spear looks like the *zhupin* of Islamic northern Iran and Afghanistan, but is more likely the result of a long-shared military tradition. In

other respects, his clothing, jewellery and hairstyle are typical of southern India during this period. In contrast, his horse's armour raises interesting questions. As yet the only other example of horse-armour in which a rider's leg disappears inside the armour, apart from its frequent representation in Hoysala art, is in immediately pre-Islamic Yemen. Might these two sources, separated by six or seven centuries and thousands of kilometres, reflect an unknown military tradition taken to medieval India by invading Arab-Islamic armies during the intervening years?

(2) Eastern Ganga commander or standard-bearer, 12th–13th centuries
The Eastern Ganga were a notably long-lasting Indian dynasty, as well as being wealthy, powerful and cultured. For much of their history they were also on the front line against Islamic expansion. Most of the military technology shown in the art of their realm is traditional and highly decorated, the harness of this man's horse – and the weaponry attached to its saddle – being typical. On the other hand, his sword with its hand-protecting guard is remarkably advanced for this period. The decorated shield shown in this reconstruction is based on a medieval Indian shield recently found as a ceiling decoration in a rock-carved church in faraway Ethiopia, but was not specifically of Ganga origin. The symbolic parasol is based upon art from several parts of India and is even more decorated than the earlier example shown in Plate C.

(3) Infantryman, south India, 12th–13th centuries
Outside of the ruling and military elites, there was considerable similarity among the ordinary soldiers of 'peninsular' southern India, at least where their varied but often limited military equipment was concerned. This man, for example, could probably have been found in the armies of a dozen dynasties. On the other hand, his sword with its slender 'waisted' blade was clearly a development of earlier Indian cutting and stabbing weapons. His substantial dagger or fighting knife is again typical, though with a notably decorated sheath and fancifully knotted sash. Meanwhile the outer surface of his shoulder-belt is almost entirely covered by rows of cowrie shells. The mantlet shield is similarly distinctive, being formed of a wooden frame with a sheet of leather, rawhide or otherwise cured animal skin nailed to the inside.

G: INDIAN ARMIES OF THE 14TH CENTURY
(1) Central Indian nobleman, 14th century
During the 14th century, several Hindu states fell to Indo-Islamic assault from the north. This period also saw an Islamization of some aspects of Hindu civilization, without any accompanying conversion to Islam, particularly within ruling courts and their armies. Thus, the clothes of this Hindu Indian nobleman differ only in details from those worn in Muslim Indian courts in which various traditional Indian fashions were correspondingly being adopted. His one-piece steel helmet is within this shared late-medieval Indian military-technological tradition, as is his decorated saddle and horse-harness, whereas the use of a snaffle rather than a curb-bit bridle might reflect the influence of Mongol invaders. The attachment of archery equipment to the saddle, rather than being attached to a rider's weapons belt, was old-fashioned, however.

(2) Elite infantry attendant from east-central India, 14th century
In contrast to the Hindu nobleman, this foot soldier from east-central India, though a member of the warrior elite, is equipped in a highly traditional manner – with one notable

exception. He carries an early form of *katar* punch-dagger, which first appeared during the 14th century and would remain a specifically Indian weapon. In contrast, his sword was imported from the Arab Middle East, while the blade attached to one corner of his rectangular wooden shield appears only occasionally in Indian art where it might have been more fanciful than real.

(3) Chieftain from Gujarat, early 14th century
The Hindu and Jain rulers of Gujarat and Rajasthan resisted Islamic conquest both militarily and culturally. Thus, this chieftain clings to several archaic styles of costume and military equipment. Whether the large fluted headgear that appears in several pictorial sources was a helmet, as interpreted here, or a ceremonial hat or crown is unclear, for no comparable objects seem to have survived. His gilded mace may have been more of a symbol of command than a practical weapon, but his massive, broad-bladed sword was a business-like piece of equipment. The muslin shawl around his body and shoulders was a specifically Indian fashion that was also adopted by the Indo-Islamic elites.

H: INDIAN ARMIES OF THE 15TH CENTURY
(1) Cavalryman from central India, mid-15th century
The Islamization of the weaponry and costume of the elites of the remaining non-Islamic states in India continued through the 15th century. Whereas Hindu, Jain or Buddhist armies of earlier centuries looked radically different from their Muslim opponents, differences were often now a matter of details, at least where cavalry forces were concerned. This man's slender-bladed war-axe could be found in Indo-Islamic central and northern India where it was known as a *nachakh*, while his partially scale-lined coif is a mixture of long-established Indian and more recent Iranian-Islamic traditions. His scale-lined cuirass with flap-like sleeves is structurally almost identical to many Islamic armours of this period, even as far west as southern Spain. The straight sword finds parallels in the Mamluk sultanate of Egypt and Syria, though less so in intervening Iran or Central Asia. His continuing use of a wooden bow and the carrying of it in an unstrung condition in a long bow-case would, however, have been regarded as very old-fashioned in most Islamic territories. In contrast, his horse's armour and harness are practically identical to those used in the Sultanate of Delhi.

(2) Hindu nobleman from south-central India, mid-15th century
The process of technological Islamization was not, of course, universal. In many parts of southern India, it was strongly resisted, at least in the portrayal of warriors and the ruling elite in art. Thus, this Hindu nobleman appears – or wishes to be portrayed – in almost ancient attire. The same was true of his weaponry, especially his bamboo bow. At first glance his slightly recurved sword appears similarly old-fashioned, but in fact it includes a modern curving knuckle-guard. The sudden appearance of this addition to a sword-hilt in Western Europe a few decades later opens up the possibility that it was brought back to Europe by early Portuguese visitors.

(3) Muslim mercenary, northern India, late 15th century
By the end of the medieval period, but before the rise of the Mughul Empire (see MAA 263 *Mughul India 1504–1761*) a distinctive style of military equipment, costume, administration, tactics and other aspects of military culture had emerged within India. This was substantially shared by India's Hindu and Muslim states, each of which made use of

A rock-cut statue of a warhorse at Konark in Orissa dating from the 13th century. (Pratishkhedekar/Wikimedia/CC BY-SA 4.0)

mercenaries, allies and subject forces who adhered to the other's religious beliefs and customs. Epitomizing such trends, this man's helmet was comparable to those seen across the late-medieval Islamic world, but with a distinctively Indian face-covering sliding nasal and cloth-covered aventail or coif. Nor would his long-hemmed, short-sleeved mail hauberk have looked out of place in Christian Europe. While his steel shield appears very Indian, his slightly curved sabre could be found as far west as the Ottoman Turkish forces invading south-eastern Europe at the time.

Undated memorial stone from Ipuru in the Guntur district of Andhra Pradesh, perhaps from the 14th century. Now held at the Government Museum, Chennai, acc. no. 2555.

INDEX

References to illustration captions are shown in **bold**. Plates are shown with page and caption locators in brackets.

Afghanistan, links with/influence of 7, **9**, 10, **13**, 19, 35, 39, 40, 41, 44, 46
Alxon-Hunnic cavalryman **9**, **A1**(25, 44)
animal skins, use of 12, 34
archers
  foot **13**, **14**, **15**, **16**, 18, **A3**(25, 44), **D2**(28, 45), 35, **42**
  mounted 16, **B2**(26, 44), **E2**(29, 46), 35–36, **37**, **38**
  seated **15**
archery equipment
  bow-cases **H1**(32, 47)
  bows and arrows **14**, 16, **16**, 18, **18**, **20**, **A3**(25, 44), **B2**(26, 44), **D2**(28, 45), **E2**(29, 46), **F2**(30, 46), **G2**(31, 46–47), **H1–2**(32, 47), 35, **37**, **38**, 42, **42**
  quivers **15**, 18, **A3**(25, 44), **B2**(26, 44), **E2**(29, 46), **G2**(31, 46–47), **H1**(32, 47), 35, **42**
armour **6**, **7**, **10**, 15, 23, **A1**(25, 44), **B1**(26, 44), **C3**(27, 45), **D1–2**(28, 45), **E2**(29, 46), **F1**(30, 46), **H1**, **3**(32, 47), 34, 38, **38**, **39**, 40–41, 44, 45, 46
  importing/sources of 22
  manufacture/storage of 22, 24, 33, 41
armouries/arsenals 33, 34
astrology, influence on warfare 14–15

Bengal infantryman **B3**(26, 44–45)
Bihar warrior **20**
blowpipes 36
boats, use of **12**
boomerangs 36

camels, use of 15, 20, **38**, **41**
caste system **3**, 6, 7, 8, 11, 12, 33, 42, 44
cattle rustling (as declaration of war) 9, 14
cavalrymen/horsemen **9**, **12**, 15, 16, 19, 20, **A1**(25, 44), **C1**(27, 45), **D1**(28, 45), **F1**(30, 46), **H1**(32, 47), **33**, **38**, **39**, **40**
chieftains **G3**(31, 47), 34, 41
China, links with/influence of 22–23, 42

daggers/fighting knives **14**, 24, **A2**(25, 44), **B1–2**(26, 44), **E2**(29, 46), **F3**(30, 46), **G1–2**(31, 46–47), 34, 36, **36**
Durga, Goddess of War **22**

Eastern Ganga forces **F2**(30, 46)
elephants, use of **9**, 14, 16–17, 18–19, **22**, **24**, **B2**(26, 44), **E2**(29, 46), 35, 36, **38**, **39**, 42
  armour/decoration of 17, 18, **22**, **24**, **B2**(26, 44), **E2**(29, 46)
  capture/taming/training 17
  mahouts 17, **B2**(26, 44), **E2**(29, 46)
  Muslim prejudice against 18–19
  trade in 10, 16

'foreign warriors' **10**
forest/hill peoples (weapons used) 36

Gond tribal warriors **E1**(29, 45–46)
Guardians of the Four Directions **16**, **17**
Gujarat cavalryman **C1**(27, 45)
Gujarat chieftain **G3**(31, 47)
Gupta warrior **10**

Hadda warrior **13**
hand-gunners 42

Harsha, King of Kashmir 11
head-coverings **D2**(28, 45), **H1**(32, 47), **41**
  caps **A2**(25, 44), **B2**(26, 44)
  helmets **6**, **7**, **9**, **10**, **11**, **A1**(25, 44), **B1**(26, 44), **C3**(27, 45), **D1**(28, 45), **G1**(31, 46), **G3**(31, 47), 38–39, **H3**(32, 47), 39–40
hero/memorial stones **3**, 13–14, **14**, **15**, **16**, **18**, **19**, **E1**(29, 45–46), **38**, **39**, **41**, 45, 46, **47**
Hindu-Shahi nobleman **B1**(26, 44)
Hinduism, and battle/warfare 12–13
horses, use of 9, **12**, 13, 14, 15, **16**, 19–20, **21**, **23**, **33**, 35, **37**, **39**, **40**, **41**, **42**, **47**
  armour/furniture **10**, **11**, 20, **21**, **23**, **A1**(25, 44), **B1**(26, 44), **C1**, **3**(27, 45), **D1**(28, 45), **F1–3**(30, 46), **G2**(31, 46–47), **H1**(32, 47), **33**, **37**, **39**, **40**, **41**, **42**, **47**
  trade in 10, 16, 19
  training of 20
Hoysala forces **E2**(29, 46), **F1**(30, 46)
hunting/huntsmen **14**, 21, 36

India
  dynastic rivalries 7–8
  external threats to 7
  trade links 22–23
Indian warfare, nature of 7–8
Indo-Iranian frontier warfare 38
Indo-Islamic armies 36, 46, 47
infantrymen/warriors **6**, **10**, 12, **13**, **14**, **19**, **20**, **A2**, **4**(25, 44), **B3**(26, 44–45), **C2**(27, 45), **E1**(29, 45–46), **F3**(30, 46), **G2**(31, 46–47), 41
'invisible weapons' **13**
Iran, links with/influence of 23, 37, 39, 42, 44, 45, 46
Islam, influence on conflicts 9

Jains 11, 18, 20, 36, 47
javelins **A2**(25, 44), **B2**(26, 44), 34, 35
jewellery **A3**(25, 44), **B3**(26, 44–45), **C3**(27, 45), **E1–2**(29, 45–46), **F1–2**(30, 46), **G1–3**(31, 46)

Kannappa Nayanar (saintly archer) **42**
Kashmir 10, 11, 23
Kashmir cavalrymen **D1**(28, 45)
kings, pre-war ceremonies of 14
Krishna **15**
Kushan warrior **10**

lances 35
lassos 36

maces **B1**(26, 44), **G3**(31, 47), 36–37
Mahmud Begada, Sultan of Gujarat 42
Mauryan warrior **6**
Middle East, military trade with 23
mlecchas, military service 11
Muhammad Ibn Qasim 10, 18
musketeers 42
Muslim mercenaries **H3**(32, 47), 36

Nandivarman II/III, King **16**
Nepal, links with 7, 45
noblemen **G1**(31, 46), **H2**(32, 47)

Orissa infantrymen **B3**(26, 44–45)
oxen, use of 16, **E3**(29, 46)

Pakistan, links with/influence of 7, 10, **14**, 19, 23, 35, 36, 44

Parantaka I, King of Chola 18
parasol-bearers/parasols **C2**(27, 45), **F2**(30, 46)
Patna warriors 41
pirates (of Bulsar), defence against 42
Pratihara commander **C3**(27, 45)

Raja Dahir 10, 18
Rajasthan 19, 20, 41, 47
Rajasthan warrior **19**
Rajput warriors 12
Rama 11
Revanta, Master of Horses **23**
rivers/roads, armies' use of 21–22

sabres **H3**(32, 47)
Sankamadeva (Kalachuri king) 38
scabbards **13**, **A1**(25, 44), **B1**(26, 44), **C1**, **3**(27, 45), **D1**(28, 45), **H1**(32, 47), 34
seals **40**
Shah Rukh 17
shields **6**, **7**, **11**, 13, **A2**, **4**(25, 44), **B1**, **3**(26, 44–45), **C2**(27, 45), **D1–2**(28, 45), **E1**(29, 45–46), **F2–3**(30, 46), **G1–3**(31, 46–47), **H1**, **3**(32, 47), **33**, 41–42, **41**, **47**
  materials used 41–42, 44
Shiva 13, **20**, 23
siege weapons 18, 36, 42
Simhavishnu, King **14**
Sindh (province) 10, 18, 19, 20
slings 36
snakeskin, use of 34
Someshvara III, King of Chalukya 20
spears **12**, **A2**(25, 44), **D1**(28, 45), **F1**(30, 46), **H3**(32, 47), 34, 35, **41**
standard-bearers **F2**(30, 46)
Surya, Sun God of Light and Daytime **17**
sword-blades 24, 34
swords **6**, **7**, **12**, **14**, **15**, **16**, **18**, **19**, **20**, **21**, **23**, **A1**, **4**(25, 44), **B1**, **3**(26, 44–45), **C1**, **3**(27, 45), **D1**(28, 45), **E1**(29, 45–46), **F2–3**(30, 46), **G1**(31, 46), **G3**(31, 47), **H1–2**(32, 47), **33**, **34**, **34**, 35, 36, **41**, 45
  decoration of **A1**(25, 44)
  importing/sources of 23
  as indicators of fortune 15, 34
  manufacture of 24, 33, 34
  symbolism of 34

throwing sticks 36
Tibet, links with/influence of 7, 22, 23, **D3**(28, 45), 39, 42
Tirmidh, attack on (704) 39
tribal warriors **E1**(29, 45–46)
Turco-Mongol influences **D1**(28, 45)
Turkish-Muslim invaders 7, 39

Veera Ballala II, King of Hoysala 38
Veerabhadra **23**
Vijayalaya Chola, King 18
Vijayanagara cavalry/infantry 15
Vijayanagara kingdom/kings 7, 15, 42
Vishnu **6**, 15

wagon drivers/wagons 16, **E3**(29, 46)
war-axes 24, **H1**(32, 47), 37–38
war-chariots/chariot corps 16
war-hammers **C3**(27, 45)
wootz steel, use of 22, 24, 34

Yemen, links with 20, 33